A Guide to Southern Utah's
Hole-in-the-Rock Trail

DESCENDANTS OF ORIGINAL HOLE-IN-THE-ROCK PIONEERS HIKE UP THE OLD TRAIL, JANUARY 1989.

A Guide
to
Southern Utah's
Hole-in-the-Rock
Trail

STEWART AITCHISON

THE UNIVERSITY
OF UTAH PRESS
Salt Lake City

To Mary and Gene Foushee

21 20 19 18 17   4 5 6

The Defiance House Man colophon is a registered trademark of the
University of Utah Press. It is based upon a four-foot-tall, Ancient
Puebloan pictograph (late PIII) near Glen Canyon, Utah.

Library of Congress Cataloging-in-Publication Data
Aitchison, Stewart W.
A guide to southern Utah's Hole-in-the-Rock Trail / Stewart Aitchison.
p. cm.
Includes bibliographical references.
ISBN 978-0-87480-821-6 (pbk. : alk. paper)
1. Hole in the Rock Trail (Utah)—Guidebooks. 2. Hole in the Rock Trail (Utah)—
History. 3. Mormon pioneers—Utah—San Juan County—History. 4. Frontier and
pioneer life—Utah—San Juan County. 5. San Juan County (Utah)—History, Local.
I. Title.
F832.S4A37 2005
917.92'59042—dc22   2004024540

Contents

Illustrations

~ Maps ~

Preface

I'm bundled up in wool, down, and nylon but am still having trouble keeping my fingers warm enough to write. A bitterly cold wind whips across the stark landscape. Below me, I can see a skiff of ice on the San Juan arm of Lake Powell. Out in the gathering darkness, a great horned owl gives a lonely hoot. It's hard to fathom the miserable conditions that pioneers faced on the trail, especially in winter.

Some had frostbitten toes and fingers—how they must have ached. Those in charge of the livestock sat astride their steeds, leaned into the relentless storms, became soaked by wet snow with absolutely no shelter, no relief. Think about the women and their babies. As the days added up to weeks and the weeks dragged into months, they worried about their little ones becoming sick and dying on the trail.

Yet these indefatigable people trusted in God and persisted in completing their mission. They didn't despair. Instead, they danced and sang and prayed.

I'm totally impressed, amazed, and cold.

— Grey Mesa, January

Acknowledgments

All of us who treasure Bluff owe a great deal to Gene and Mary Foushee, Bluff "pioneers" who arrived in the 1950s to build the Recapture Lodge and ended up rescuing and restoring many of Bluff City's historic structures. Thank you for your vision, wonderful stories, and inspiration that led me down this particular trail. Today, the Hole-in-the-Rock Foundation, spearheaded by Corinne Roring, is carrying on this tradition by renovating the old Joseph Barton cabin, protecting the remains of the Kumen Jones house, building replicas of some of the early buildings of Bluff, and providing interpretive signs and brochures.

I must also acknowledge the late David E. Miller's classic study, *Hole-in-the-Rock*, which is the major scholarly reference about the San Juan Mission. First published in 1959 and still in print, it is the seminal work about this expedition. Without his determination and exemplary research skills, much of the story would have been lost.

For reading earlier drafts or providing useful information or both, I would like to thank Hole-in-the-Rock Trail expert Lamont Crabtree; Dale Davidson of the Monticello Bureau of Land Management (BLM) Field Office; Gene and Mary Foushee; archaeologists Winston B. Hurst and Joe Pachak; Marian Jacklin, Heritage Program manager for the Dixie National Forest; historians Steven K. Madsen and Jerry Roundy; Craig Sorenson and Barbara Sharrow, both of the Escalante Interagency Office; and John Ritenour of the Glen Canyon National Recreation Area. Donna Jordan and Jaynee Levy of the Moab and Price BLM Field Offices, respectively, helped with information on the Old Spanish Trail. LaVerne Tate of the San Juan Historical Commission and Ron McDonald located the wonderful historic photos for my use.

I am also grateful for all the help received from Bill Frank of the Huntington Library; Raynelda Calderon of the New York Public Library; Jenny Presnell of the Miami University Library; Rick Reese of the

University of Utah; Helen Hoopes and Russ Taylor, both of the Brigham Young University Library; Doug Misner of the Utah History Information Center; and historian Dwight Smith. Thanks to all of you for ferreting out obscure bits of information for me.

Thanks, too, to Jim and LuAnn Hook, current owners of the Recapture Lodge, and Liza Doran, owner of the Cow Canyon Trading Post, for their hospitality.

For many pleasant days on the trail, I must extend my appreciation to Larry Sanford, Marty Sewell, Bill Williams, and my wife, Ann, and daughter, Kate. Peter DeLafosse, the rest of the University of Utah Press staff, and Annette Wenda get the credit for putting all the pieces together.

History is not an exact science. Different versions arise from different perspectives and the effect of time on memories. It is my hope that this book comes reasonably close to the true story of the San Juan Mission. Except where noted in the text, I have used place-name spellings as they appear on current United States Geological Survey (USGS) maps. Any errors of fact are strictly my responsibility.

Disclaimer

Neither the author nor the publisher assumes any liability for injury, damage to property, or violation of the law that may arise from using this book. Use of this book indicates the reader's assumption that it may contain errors.

As you traverse these roads and trails in southern Utah, please be mindful of a strange but wonderful living crust growing on much of the high desert soil. This lumpy black crust is known variously as cryptobiotic soil or microbiotic crust. It consists of different species of lichens, mosses, cyanobacteria (blue-green algae), liverworts, algae, and microfungi. These fragile living crusts help stabilize the soil, increase water absorption, and add nitrogen and carbon to the soil. Unfortunately, walking or driving on these crusts breaks them apart and the underlying soil weathers away. Please stay on established trails.

The paved sections are open all year except possibly following a heavy snowstorm. The unpaved sections are open seasonally. Always check locally for current road conditions.

The maps in this book should be used only for general planning. The latest USGS maps should be consulted for exploring the trail.

Hole-in-the-Rock viewed from lake powell.

1

Impossible Journey

We have heard much about the difficulties of the overland trail from the Missouri to the Pacific, but countless caravans traveled half the continent in less time than it took these Saints to cross the corner of one state. On all the overland trails there was not one obstacle comparable to what they conquered at Grand Gulch, the Slick Rocks, Clay Hills, or Comb Wash, to say nothing of Hole-in-the-Rock.

—David Lavender, historian

~ February 1, 1880 ~

With tears welling up in his eyes, little Willie Decker cried, "How will we ever get home again?" He and his mother, Elizabeth, had just scrambled down the infamous Hole-in-the-Rock, a natural crack widened in a sandstone cliff that barely accommodated a wagon, and then had made their way along Uncle Ben's Dugway, a road literally tacked onto the side of the vertical cliff—a clever engineering feat. But little did they suspect that the journey to their new home in remote southeastern Utah was only half over.

The members of the Cornelius Decker family were only four of more than 230 people who had heeded the call of the Church of Jesus Christ of Latter-day Saints (LDS), the Mormons, to pull up stakes and move to the distant San Juan country of southeastern Utah, ostensibly to start a farming community. However, the San Juan Mission (its official name but later more commonly known as the Hole-in-the-Rock Expedition) would unwittingly become one of the most extraordinary wagon trips ever undertaken in North America.

It was the last major wagon train in the United States, the only emigrant train to go west to east, one of the few that actually gained in numbers (two babies born along the way survived), and one of the slowest (with a daily average of less than two miles, even slower than the Mormon handcart companies that crossed middle America from Iowa and Nebraska to Utah). And though the trail that these devoted pioneers scratched from the raw frontier was used for several years afterward, no highway was built over most of the route because it was deemed just too rugged for modern vehicles.

This guide explores the historic Hole-in-the-Rock Trail, gives insight into this remarkable accomplishment, and points out some of the fascinating natural history along the way. So slip on your boots, fasten your chaps, pull down your Stetson, and grab the reins for a ride through time and space in what is still some of the most inaccessible country in the United States.

2

The Call

December 1878 to March 1879

The Mormons, led by Brigham Young, had arrived in the Great Salt Lake Valley in 1847. Soon afterward, Young began a colonization program that would include not only the Utah Territory but also much of the Intermountain West and extend to the Pacific coast of California and beyond to foreign countries. When Young died thirty years later, he had directed the colonization efforts of more than three hundred settlements in the West. Most of the Utah region contained at least a scattering of small towns, farms, and ranches. However, one notable exception was the southeastern corner of the territory. This forsaken, trackless land of sandstone gorges, high mesas, and little water was separated from the rest of Utah by the deep canyons carved by the Colorado River and its tributaries. Church leaders feared that the remote corner would be taken over by outlaws and "Gentiles" (non-Mormons), plus it served as a refuge for renegade Navajos, Paiutes, and Utes who continued to prey upon the Mormon settlements.

Morgan Amasa Barton, son of Joseph F. Barton, one of the leaders of the San Juan Mission, wrote that southeastern Utah was "a point of interception of bank robbers, horse thieves, cattle rustlers, jail breakers, train robbers, and general desperadic criminals." And an 1861 Utah newspaper article added that it was "one vast continuity of waste and measurably valueless, excepting for nomadic purposes, hunting grounds for Indians, and to hold the world together."

After the nineteenth century gold and silver rushes in Colorado, hopeful prospectors wandered down toward southeastern Utah looking for their El Dorado and the legendary secret silver mine of the Navajo. Texas cowboys followed the prospectors, searching for new rangelands to raise beef to sell to the miners—just like they had done in Colorado.

The late 1870s was also a time of increasing antagonism between Mormons and non-Mormons because of a federal campaign to eliminate plural marriage and to take political control of Salt Lake City and the Utah Territory. The church wanted to lay claim to all the water and farming land in southeastern Utah before others could.

The Native Americans already living in the area grew increasingly concerned over the invasion of outsiders. A few of the Indians raided outlying Mormon settlements and drove stolen stock southeast of the Colorado River. Albert R. Lyman, a descendant of the Hole-in-the-Rock pioneers, claims that in 1867 more than a million dollars' worth of horses, cattle, and sheep was looted from the Utah frontier.

One objective of the San Juan Mission was to cultivate better relations with the Indians. Brigham Young had always believed that it was "cheaper to feed than to fight them." Additionally, church doctrine taught that the Indians were descendants of the House of Israel who had strayed from the righteous life but would eventually embrace the gospel and become a "white and delightsome" people.

Probably at a conference held in St. George in 1878, the idea for a mission into southeastern Utah was born. The exact location for a new colony had not been determined, just vaguely somewhere in what is today called the Four Corners country, where the four states of Colorado, New Mexico, Utah, and Arizona meet. Southwestern Utah communities, being closest to the area, would be expected to supply most of the colonists.

A "mission call" went out to a dozen southwestern Utah communities on December 28 and 29, 1878, from the Quarterly Conference held in the Parowan meetinghouse. At the following March 22 and 23 quarterly meeting, more names were announced. Still no specific site had been selected, and not all called up were to go to the Four Corners area; some were destined for east-central Arizona, Nevada, or elsewhere.

The church elders planned for a community in southeastern Utah to act as a buffer against those whom they saw as troublemakers. As had been done many times before, the call was for "volunteers." In

Figure 1. Silas S. Smith was the official leader of the San Juan Mission. Courtesy of Ron McDonald.

truth, church leaders made a list of the people they thought would be appropriate to accomplish this goal. People with particular skills for establishing a community were placed on the list. Parowan bishop C. J. Arthur reminded them that they were not compelled to go, "but advised all who were called to go with a cheerful heart."

Nearly all accepted not only willingly but also with great enthusiasm. Single men were advised to seek brides and marry since this colonization was intended to be a permanent project, and families would help ensure this goal. A few, including some non-LDS people, who were not on the list attached themselves to the group, not as part of the mission but simply to travel to Colorado or elsewhere in the relative safety of a larger group.

Silas S. Smith Sr., a member of the Legislative Council, was appointed the "presiding officer" of the proposed expedition. President Smith had long advocated for a colony along the San Juan River, and he now had the opportunity to attempt to create one.

3

The Exploration
April 14 to Mid-September 1879

Besides packing their belongings and necessary supplies, the most important order of business was deciding exactly where this new town was going to be. For this task, an exploratory party, the San Juan Exploring Company, was put together consisting of twenty-six (or twenty-seven) men, two women, and eight children. Silas S. Smith was made captain. They took with them a dozen wagons, about eighty horses, and perhaps two hundred cattle, plus six months' worth of supplies. (Other accounts list fewer wagons and livestock.) On April 14, 1879, the party set out from Paragonah in search of a new home.

The exploring party made their way east from Paragonah, settled in 1852, by going up Little Creek, over a pass, and down through Bear Valley, which joins Sevier Valley on a well-established wagon road along part of the Old Spanish Trail. The party then turned south off the Old Spanish Trail to the farming town of Panguitch, established in 1864. Here locals John Butler and Hamilton Thornton joined them.

Southeast of Panguitch, a wagon road paralleled the Sevier River to its West Fork head. A short distance beyond, the road turned southeast toward upper Kanab Creek then went down Johnson Canyon to its mouth, where the pioneers encountered the Honeymoon Trail. Turning east, they passed Navajo Well, then went southeast over Buckskin Mountain and down House Rock Valley to House Rock Spring.

The wagons had to be "lowered by ropes" to get them off Buckskin Mountain. (It's not clear if this meant disassembling the wagons or just using ropes to hold the wagons back.) At House Rock Spring, Robert Bullock, Edward F. Davis, John T. Gower, Thomas S. Bladen, George Urie, Kumen Jones, and James J. Adams left their names on the rocks along with the date "Apr. 25, 79."

The trail skirted around the base of the Vermilion Cliffs. The group camped at Jacob's Pool, Soap Creek, and Badger Creek, finally arriving at Lee's Ferry on April 30, but not before George Urie and John Gower's wagon broke an axle at Soap Creek, which was temporarily replaced with a cottonwood log but abandoned at the ferry.

John Doyle Lee had been instructed by the Mormon Church to start a ferry operation at the head of the Grand Canyon in 1872. This remote location also served as a hideout for Lee, who was implicated in the tragic Mountain Meadows Massacre in which more than one hundred members of a wagon train were killed in 1857 by a group of Mormons and Southern Paiutes.

The exploring party was ferried across the Colorado River and climbed up a dugway onto the rough tilted bench known as Lee's Backbone, which led south along the base of the towering Echo Cliffs. Water was scarce and what could be found of poor quality. The known watering places were Navajo Spring, Bitter Spring, Limestone Tank, and Willow Springs. It was more than thirty hot, dusty miles between Limestone Tank and Willow Springs, and George Hobbs claimed that a quarter of the cattle perished along this stretch. They camped from May 3 to May 7 near Willow Springs, and someone left the inscription "Ma 7 1879" along with some now illegible names.

Finally, they reached the Hopi pueblo of Moenkopi, where several years before a small farming community of Mormons had been established. Here the exploratory party found John W. Young constructing a mill to process wool from Navajo flocks. The exploring company stayed about a week, resting, repairing wagons and other gear, shoeing horses,

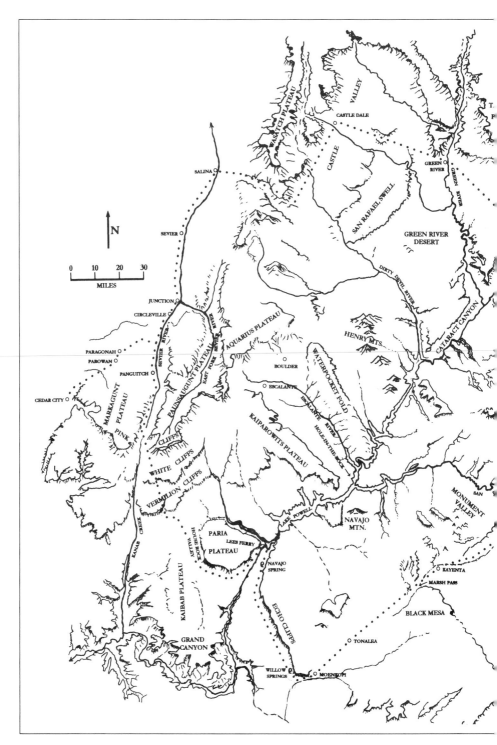

Map 1. ROUTE OF SAN JUAN EXPLORING COMPANY.

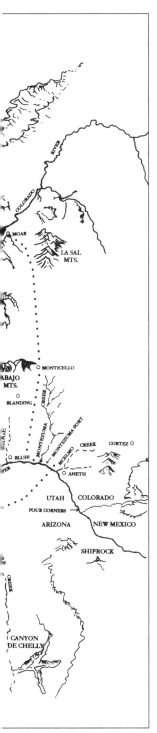

and earning some Indian corn by helping Young. Wagons had never gone northeast from Moenkopi, so a road would have to be built. The settlers at Moenkopi tried to dissuade the explorers from continuing their journey across Navajo land.

Unfazed by these warnings, the explorers hired Seth Tanner, later instrumental in the building the Tanner Trail in the eastern Grand Canyon, and an unidentified Navajo to guide them to the San Juan River. Thales Haskell also joined the group.

Because of the poor condition of the cattle and the risk of losing them to Indians, Captain Smith ordered that all loose stock be left at Moenkopi until the road was completed. The James L. Davis family decided to stay here, too, but the Harrison H. Harriman family chose to continue.

On May 13, the party left their friends and followed Moenkopi Wash toward Tonalea or Red Lake, which was dry. By digging in the wash, water was obtained. Finding water continued to be a major problem, and the Navajos encountered were not eager to share it. Adding to the tension was the fact that Navajos had killed Mormon missionary George A. Smith Jr. near here in 1860.

Their route then passed Elephant Feet, strange stone pillars, continuing to Cow Springs. Here, too, digging wells produced water. On the eighth day, they went through Marsh Pass and camped in the vicinity of Tsegi Canyon. At Kayenta a natural sandstone tank was found where thousands of Navajo sheep were being watered. The color of the water was the same as that found in a corral, but the brethren had no choice but to drink it.

They followed Laguna Wash downstream and on May 23 camped in the vicinity of Dennehotso with a group of Paiutes and Navajos. Peeaga-ment, an old Paiute, demanded five hundred dollars before the train could pass through his country. Smith ignored him and instructed the party to give small gifts such as tobacco and food, especially to the In-dian children. It wasn't long until the Paiutes were friendly and Peeaga-ment lost his bluster.

A couple of days later, as the party was making its way down Chinle Wash, Nielson B. Dalley's mare accidentally kicked Smith's horse, breaking its leg. Smith had to shoot the injured animal. Within minutes, some Navajos had the horse butchered and roasting on a fire.

Over the next five days, they worked their way out of Chinle Wash, across miles of deep sand and bare rock, camped at Lost Spring, and traveled through Chimney Wash to Cave Springs then through more dunes to Alkali Gulch. Smith climbed Boundary Butte with "a glass to look out the way."

On Saturday, May 31, the main party reached the south bank of the San Juan River across from Allen's Bottom. On the opposite shore were the Mitchells, John Brewer, and George Clay—all non-Mormons from Colorado who had arrived the previous year to farm along the river, be-tween Montezuma Creek and McElmo Wash.

The San Juan was swollen with the spring runoff from the southern Rockies, and the party spent two days looking for a safe crossing and, no doubt, observing the odd phenomenon called sand waves, which are pe-culiar to heavily silted fast-flowing rivers. The surface water traveling faster than the bottom current suddenly creates waves many feet in height.

Once across, Smith visited Peter Shirts, who had arrived several years earlier from southern Utah and was the only Mormon living along the lower San Juan. Shirts lived in a cabin near where Montezuma Creek entered the San Juan. The next day, Smith went to visit the Mitchells, who, like Shirts, were discouraged at trying to get the unruly San Juan to irrigate instead of wash away their fields.

In the meantime, the others explored up and down the river for suitable farmland. Smith and the party placed their initial camp about three miles upstream from the Mitchells, which was just below the confluence of McElmo Creek and the San Juan. Here they all decided to build a dam on the river in an attempt to control its flow and divert water to irrigate their fields, including the land belonging to the folks from Colorado and Shirts. In return, the first settlers offered to share their crops with the new arrivals.

On June 17, the brethren went to the Mitchells' place to attend the wedding of Clara M. Mitchell and Mr. Willians (spelling from historic diary) performed by a Presbyterian minister from Mancos, Colorado. No doubt, this was the first marriage between white people on the lower San Juan.

While work continued on the dam, some of the men headed for Colorado, ending up going all the way to Alamosa, more than four hundred miles round-trip, to obtain supplies. Others explored the country around the Abajo Mountains, locally called the Blues, and four others returned to Moenkopi to bring the Davis family and remaining livestock. During their trip, they had a run-in with an Indian named Peoken who may have been responsible for the killing of George A. Smith Jr.

When the Davis family arrived on July 17 at what was magnanimously being called Montezuma Fort—really just several primitive cabins—about one mile upstream from Shirts's cabin, a very pregnant Mary Elizabeth Davis bemoaned that this was a terribly isolated place. About two weeks later, she had a baby girl, christened Ethel, the first white child born in southeastern Utah.

All possible farmland was claimed from above McElmo Wash down to Butler Wash. Log houses were built, including some just a mile upstream of present-day Bluff.

The finished two hundred-foot-long dam, made of logs, stones, sticks, and mud, raised the river level three feet. Unfortunately, the snowmelt from the mountains quickly subsided, and little if any water ran down the irrigation ditches. By late summer, everyone's crops had failed, "burned up for lack of water."

Regardless of the hardships, time was made for regular church services on Sunday mornings and Sacrament meetings in the evenings. Fourth of July and Pioneer Day (July 24, the day Brigham Young first entered the Salt Lake Valley in 1847) were celebrated.

By the middle of August, the explorers were ready to return to southwestern Utah, some to bring back their families, others having decided not to live in this wild place. The Harriman and Davis families and Harvey Dunton remained at Montezuma Fort. John Gower and George Urie went back via Moenkopi to Lee's Ferry to retrieve their broken wagon, but the rest wanted to avoid the troublesome Indians and decided to return to the settlements via the Old Spanish Trail. But no wagon road existed north between Montezuma Fort and the Old Spanish Trail.

Preceded by a few scouts and road builders, the majority of the party left Montezuma Fort on August 19. First, they went downstream along the north bank of the San Juan, then turned up Recapture Wash toward the foot of the Abajo Mountains, passing near the present sites of Blanding and Monticello. They continued northward until encountering the Old Spanish Trail southwest of the La Sal Mountains. They crossed the Colorado River where Moab is now located.

The trail angled northwest and crossed the Green River (about two and a half miles north of the present town of Green River), then went toward Castle Dale, then south around the southern part of the Wasatch Plateau and dropped into Salina Canyon, which the party then followed to Sevier Valley. They then went up the Sevier River until they met their earlier route north of Panguitch.

It was mid-September when they returned to Paragonah. This exploratory trip had covered nearly a thousand miles and resulted in the building of several hundred miles of wagon road. Most important, a site for the San Juan Mission had been discovered. However, there still remained the question of how to get the colonists there quickly and safely.

The southern route was deemed too dangerous considering the resentful attitude of the Navajos and Paiutes plus the problems of locating enough water and feed for the livestock. And the northern route over the Old Spanish Trail was thought to be too long. Why travel 450 miles to reach a point less than 200 miles due east?

Winter was quickly approaching, and the colonists wanted to reach the San Juan and build cabins before the severest cold weather blew in. Lying almost in a direct line between Parowan and Montezuma Fort was the town of Escalante, established in Potato Valley in 1876. A wagon road existed that far, and the remaining 125 miles or so shouldn't be a problem. (Some historians speculate that if Brigham Young had still been alive, he would not have allowed a wagon train to depart on an unscouted route.)

This reasoning was further bolstered by favorable reports from Escalante residents Charles Hall, Andrew P. Schow, and Reuben Collett. These three men had been sent out by the church to locate a suitable crossing of the Colorado River. Hall reported: "It would be something of a problem to get wagons down to the river, but once down and across, it would be a simple matter to move on to the San Juan, about sixty miles away."

During the summer of 1879, Schow and Collett had taken a wagon box boat mounted on a two-wheeled cart to the canyon rim above the Colorado. After examining the narrow notch that would become the infamous Hole-in-the-Rock, they went upstream along the rim to a point near where the Escalante River empties into the Colorado River. They slid the boat down to a narrow, grassy bench (Jackass Bench, now

Figure 2. Although originally appointed as the San Juan Mission assistant leader, Platte D. Lyman became the de facto field captain after leader Silas S. Smith returned to Salt Lake City and was unable to rejoin the mission until the spring of 1880. Courtesy of the San Juan Historical Commission.

submerged at high pool under Lake Powell, created in 1963) and then over a precipice to the Colorado. Using two boards as paddles, they stroked across and climbed out of the canyon until they could see the San Juan in the distance. They returned to report that they believed "a good road could be made" to take the colonists to the San Juan. However, they must have gone only as far as to see the San Juan River gorge, not the river itself. Otherwise, they would have realized how tortuous the country was a few miles east of the Colorado.

The mission leaders, including President Smith, decided on an Escalante "shortcut"—a fateful decision. The wagon train would go to Escalante and from there in a straight line to Montezuma Fort. Platte D. Lyman was chosen as Smith's assistant.

✠ Following the Trail ✠

Today, St. George, Cedar City, and Parowan are all connected by Interstate 15, which closely follows part of the historic Old Spanish Trail. The thousand-mile-long Old Spanish Trail once connected Santa Fe with Los Angeles and was most active between 1829 and 1848. Despite its name, it was primarily used by Mexican caravans, Indians, and other non-Spanish travelers. The exploratory party took the Old Spanish Trail from Parowan through Paragonah to the Sevier Valley.

To follow the exploratory route, start in Parowan and drive northeast 4 miles to Paragonah. One-half mile north of Paragonah, turn right (east) onto a gravel road that heads toward the Hurricane Cliffs. The road, Forest Road 077, climbs into the Dixie National Forest following

Little Creek, which is lined with narrow-leaf cottonwood and dense stands of Gamble oak and punctuated with an occasional beaver pond.

About 7.3 miles from Paragonah, turn left (north) and go past Aspen Spring and over the 8,100-foot pass. In another 6.2 miles there is an interesting half-mile side trip to the Forest Service Guard Station, where Holyoak Spring still issues from the base of a low hill. But watch out for the prolific stinging nettle. Another 8.3 miles down Bear Creek Valley, pavement is again reached at UT 20.

Turn right (southeast) and drive 7.2 miles to U.S. 89, which runs down Sevier Valley. Turn right again (south) and drive 10.1 miles to Panguitch. Continue south on U.S. 89 to the head of the West Fork of the Sevier River at Long Valley Junction. Thirty-two miles from Panguitch, turn left (east) to Alton and follow the well-signed dirt roads 39.8 miles to and through Johnson Canyon. Watch for elk! Turn left (east) back onto U.S. 89. Go 9.4 miles and turn right (south) onto the dirt road BLM 715.

The spider web of dusty tracks can be confusing but is fairly well marked with signs for the Honeymoon Trail, which received its name after 1877 when the St. George Temple was completed and young Mormon couples from Arizona began traveling north to have their marriages sealed there. These travelers planted trees such as Lombardy poplars and Fremont cottonwoods at springs along the trail.

In about 4 miles, the road enters Arizona and becomes BLM 1025 and begins to climb into dense pinyon pinejuniper woodland. After another 16 miles, the road drops down the rocky East Kaibab Monocline, a great fold in the earth's crust, into House Rock Valley and the junction with BLM 1065. Turn right (south) and drive 15 miles to paved U.S. 89A.

To visit the House Rock Spring camp, 4 miles north of U.S. 89A, turn east onto a private road. Stop at the house and ask permission to cross the owners' property before proceeding. About 1 mile farther, the road ends, but it is a short walk on a trail to the spring area. You may also see the recently reintroduced California condors soaring above the Vermilion Cliffs.

Back at U.S. 89A, turn left (east) toward Marble Canyon, the head of the Grand Canyon. A historical marker at milepost 557 tells about the history of this route. Before crossing the Marble Canyon bridge over the Colorado River, take the 6-mile road down to Lee's Ferry, which is where the exploratory party crossed the mighty Colorado. The ferry crossing and a number of historic buildings are now part of Glen Canyon National Recreation Area. From the House Rock Valley Road to the Marble Canyon bridge is 28 miles.

Back at the bridge, the Marble Canyon Visitor Center offers books, maps, and information about the area. Once across the bridge, you enter the vast Navajo Indian Reservation.

Continue south on U.S. 89A along the base of the Echo Cliffs 51 miles to Indian Route 23, a dirt road. As you go along, notice the relatively green oases of Navajo Spring (now a highway maintenance yard) and Bitter Spring. As you reach the southern end of the Echo Cliffs, note that the old trail stayed closer to them than the modern highway.

Turn left (southeast) onto Indian Route 23. To the northeast, notice the tall cottonwoods and Lombardy poplars growing against the Echo Cliffs at Willow Springs. Along the next 8 miles, the road follows part of the ancient Hopi Salt Trail that led from the Hopi country to shrines and mineral deposits in the Little Colorado River Gorge and the Grand Canyon. More greenery is evident at the small settlement of Moenave, and just before reaching U.S. 160 there are some signed fossilized dinosaur tracks.

Turn left (east) onto U.S. 160 and drive 5.4 miles to Tuba City. Make a right turn at the stoplight in Tuba to visit Moenkopi. Otherwise, continue 126 miles northeast on U.S. 160 through Kayenta to Red Mesa. Turn left (north) onto Indian Route 35 and drive 35 miles to the settlement of Montezuma Creek.

Montezuma Fort, a collection of primitive cabins, was located approximately one-half mile downstream (west) of the San Juan bridge on Indian Route 35. The fort was washed away in the floods of 1884, but historian Ron McDonald may have discovered its remains in the present San Juan River channel. See his article "Fort Montezuma."

From Montezuma Creek, take UT 163 14 miles west to U.S. 191, then turn right (north). After 58 miles, about 8 miles south of La Sal Junction, the highway meets the Old Spanish Trail and roughly follows it another 32 miles to Moab. Continue across the Colorado River 29 miles north to Interstate 70, which you then take west 32.8 miles to the town of Green River. The original trail angled more northwesterly than the modern highway to reach the Green River crossing, which was about 2.5 miles north of the present town. Be sure to visit the John Wesley Powell River History Museum in Green River.

Continue west and at Interstate 70 exit 156 take U.S. 191/U.S. 6 north about 17 miles. Turn left (west) onto the dirt Buckhorn Flat Road, also known as the Green River Cutoff, which leads about 48 miles through the northern end of the San Rafael Swell to Castle Dale and UT 10. The old railroad grade, built in 1880–1883 by the Denver & Rio Grande Western, parallels the Old Spanish Trail around the northern end of the swell. In this area there are a number of variations to the Old Spanish Trail, but this is a good approximation.

From Castle Dale to Salina, drive UT 10 37 miles south to Interstate 70 and follow it 38 miles west to Salina.

From Salina to Sevier the exploratory party followed the Sevier River. Stay on Interstate 70 for 35 miles and get off at exit 23, at Sevier. From the town of Sevier continue 52 miles south on U.S. 89 to the junction with UT 20, then turn right (west).

At this point, you have completed the circle. Follow, in reverse, the above directions to return to Paragonah. Incidentally, about 3.3 miles south of Circleville on the west side of the highway is the boyhood cabin of outlaw Robert Leroy Parker (Butch Cassidy).

4

The Wagon Train Begins

Mid-October to November 1879

While the exploring party was away, the colonists spent the summer preparing for the journey. Homes and farms, large machinery, furniture, and other bulky goods had to be sold or disposed of. Herds of cattle and horses had to be rounded up. A typical wagon bed was four feet wide and ten to twelve feet long. Into it had to be packed clothing, cooking gear, food (at least six weeks' worth, some taking double that amount), bedding, tents, seed grain, weaponry, iron stoves, tools, extra parts, furniture, first aid supplies, repair equipment, and perhaps a few luxuries such as musical instruments. All these items could weigh a ton or more. Draft animals were needed, too. Some preferred oxen to mules; they were cheaper, could graze off the land, and could be slaughtered and eaten if need be.

Most people were ready by mid-October when announcement of the Escalante "shortcut" came. Since participants were coming from various parts of southwestern Utah and starting at slightly different times, instructions went out that a general rendezvous point would be made somewhere in the desert southeast of Escalante. Fortymile Spring became this point not because of previous planning but because the country beyond that spot presented obstacles too great for an individual or small group to handle.

Figure 3. WAGONS WERE LOADED WITH EVERYTHING NEEDED TO START A NEW LIFE IN
SOUTHEASTERN UTAH. MOST PEOPLE PACKED ONLY ENOUGH FOOD FOR A SIX-WEEK OR
SO JOURNEY. LITTLE DID THEY SUSPECT THAT THE TRIP WOULD TAKE THE ENTIRE WIN-
TER AND THEY WOULD BE REDUCED TO EATING GROUND SEED WHEAT, PARCHED CORN,
AND AN OCCASIONAL PIECE OF BEEF.

From Paragonah to Panguitch, the pioneers followed the same well-
established wagon road as the earlier exploring party. Up Little Creek
Canyon, past Aspen Spring, over the pass into Bear Valley to Holyoak
Spring (also known as Bear Spring; on the USGS topographic map it is
mislabeled as Holly Oak Spring and according to George W. Decker is
"the best water in the world") and then to the Sevier River and south to
Panguitch.

One of the largest contingents was from the Cedar City vicinity with
Jens Nielson in charge. At fifty-nine, Nielson was one of the oldest
members and became the unofficial patriarch of the San Juan Mission.
He had already built homes in Parowan, Paragonah, Panguitch, and
Cedar City when he was called up for this mission. Originally from Den-
mark, he was a member of the ill-fated 1856 Willie Handcart Company.
While crossing the Great Plains, his young son died and Jens froze his

Figure 4. The ruins of the Widtsoe School House stand in mute testimony to one lonely outpost that didn't last.

Figure 5. The settlement of Escalante was established in 1876 and was the last town before the San Juan Mission pioneers headed out into the unknown.

feet, which necessitated hauling him along with the family's belongings in the cart. Walking was painful for the rest of his life.

While resting at Holyoak Spring Camp, the expedition was formally organized. The Cedar City contingent combined with people from Parowan and Paragonah. This train of wagons and cattle stretched almost two miles. Members were assigned various duties and tasks from collecting firewood to locating springs and repairing the road. Some of the younger single men were put in charge of the livestock. Campfire meetings were conducted and included singing, readings, speeches, and gospel sermons. The singing was accompanied by violin, accordion, trumpet, cornet, and Jew's harp. Dancing was popular wherever level ground or smooth rock could be found. The horn instruments also called the camp together for morning and evening prayers and signaled the beginning of the day's march.

From Panguitch, they followed another established wagon route through Red Canyon to the top of the Paunsaugunt Plateau and then along the East Fork of the Sevier River to the Riddle Ranch (in the vicinity of Widtsoe). They then faced a fairly steep climb to the head of Sweetwater Canyon into the Escalante Mountains, an extension of the lofty Aquarius Plateau. Sweetwater Spring was another major campsite.

While crossing the 9,300-foot pass, a snowstorm hit, and the people and teams struggled through deep snow and mud. Henry John Holyoak froze his toes while driving stock. From the summit, they had their first view of Fiftymile Mountain (Kaiparowits Plateau) and the wild desert beyond Escalante. As they descended nearly 3,500 feet off the mountain into Potato Valley, the weather and road conditions improved. Escalante was the last town and near the end of any semblance of a wagon road.

Some of the missionaries complained that in Escalante prices for goods such as flour, potatoes, and sorghum were unreasonably high but most commended the townspeople for their generosity. A baby was stillborn or died shortly after birth, which was possibly premature, while the

Figure 6. THE VAST KAIPAROWITS PLATEAU STRETCHES FOR FIFTY MILES FROM ESCALANTE TO THE RIM OF GLEN CANYON.

group was in Escalante. The child was probably not named before burial and thus was not considered a casualty of the journey.

Beyond Escalante, cattlemen had been using the range for several years, and a wagon road extended down Alvey Wash to about as far as Tenmile Spring, so-called because it was about ten miles from town. For many miles, relatively flat but sandy desert is squeezed between the Straight Cliffs of Fiftymile Mountain and the Escalante River drainage system. Finding adequate water and forage was a constant problem, but fortunately seeps and springs were discovered about ten miles apart—a good day's wagon travel. Not all of these water sources were very good, and some dried up as time passed. Samuel Rowley complained that the water at Tenmile Spring "was so hard that peas and beans would not cook in it."

Camps were made five miles south of town and at Tenmile Spring, Twentymile Wash (today Collett Wash), and Thirtymile Hollow (Coyote Gulch).

Figure 7. STRANGE ROCK FORMATIONS HAUNT DEVIL'S GARDEN.

Figure 8. FORTYMILE SPRING, NOW DEVELOPED BY RANCHERS, WAS THE INITIAL MAIN GATHERING PLACE FOR THE SAN JUAN MISSION MEMBERS IN NOVEMBER 1879.

Figure 9. AT DANCE HALL ROCK, EROSION HAS CARVED A NATURAL AMPHITHEATER COMPLETE WITH A DANCE FLOOR WHERE TRAIL-WEARY PIONEERS OCCASIONALLY HELD DANCES AND CAMP MEETINGS.

Figure 10. A SECTION OF ORIGINAL WAGON TRAIL CAN BE SEEN NEAR FORTYMILE SPRING. FEEL FREE TO WALK ALONG IT, BUT PLEASE DON'T USE VEHICLES OR BICYCLES.

By the latter part of November, most had reached Fortymile Spring, the end of the easy trail making and the rendezvous point, which would become their major headquarters for more than three weeks. President Silas S. Smith, his assistant, Platte D. Lyman, and a small party from Oak City arrived on November 27. The San Juan Mission numbers had swollen to more than 230 souls (one historian's count is 234 individuals from sixteen different Utah communities—about half being children, of which at least a dozen were under one year of age; after all, it was going to be short trip). With so many people, they had to supplement the meager springwater by melting snow. Nearly four weeks of the expected six had slipped away, and the roughest country was still ahead.

Although facing many hardships, the pioneers made time for relaxation and prayer. About a mile and a half northwest of Fortymile Spring is Dance Hall Rock, a large sandstone dome of rock with a flat, smooth bench in front leading back under a graceful overhang. On free evenings, they danced many a Welsh jig, Virginia reel, Scottish reel, polka, minuet, or schottische (a form of round dance) to the accompaniment of fiddle music. As customary, regular Latter-day Saint religious services were held on Thursday evenings and on Sunday.

But rumors were beginning to spread that the land ahead was so rough and dissected by canyons that building a road across it would be impossible. And to reach the Colorado River would mean a thousand-foot descent through a narrow crack in a vertical cliff. Dread spread through the camp.

✦ Following the Trail ✦

See the previous chapter for driving directions from Parowan to Panguitch.

From Panguitch, drive U.S. 89 7 miles south to the junction with UT 12, then turn left (east). A roadside kiosk at the mouth of spectacular Red Canyon explains some of the features of the area. A few miles up the road is the Red Canyon Visitor Center. Running parallel to the highway is a paved bike path where the pioneer wagons creaked along.

From U.S. 89 through Red Canyon to the Bryce Canyon National Park turnoff is 13.5 miles. After topping out of Red Canyon at 7,619 feet, the road crosses the broad sagebrush flat. Watch for pronghorn and endangered Utah prairie dogs. Visiting Bryce is certainly a treat, but to follow the pioneer trail, turn left (north) onto the Widtsoe Road (UT 22), paralleling the East Fork of the Sevier River.

About 13.6 miles away is Widtsoe Junction. Turn right (east) onto gravel Forest Road 17. Apostle John Widtsoe established a community here in 1910, but it was abandoned during the 1930s. A few historic but empty buildings still stand. Forest Road 17 enters the Dixie National Forest as the road gains elevation. Sagebrush is replaced first by junipers and then quickly by mixed coniferous forest. About 6 miles from Widtsoe, watch for a log fence on the right (south side), which protects Sweetwater Spring and its little stream. Here grow aspen, willow, wild rose, Oregon grape, ponderosa pine, Douglas fir, spruce, and alpine juniper—a lovely, verdant spot during the summer.

The road crosses over the 9,302-foot Escalante Summit. To the east is hauntingly beautiful, wild quintessential slickrock country. In 1866, on the trail of hostile Paiutes, Adjutant F. B. Wooley of the St. George Militia reached the edge of the Aquarius Plateau and looked out across "a naked, barren plain of red and white sandstone, crossed in all directions by innumerable gorges."

The forest road follows Birch Creek down through Main Canyon, past gray-weathered cabins slowly decaying back into the soil, to pavement again at UT 12, 22.3 miles from Widtsoe Junction. Drive another 4 miles to the hamlet of Escalante. Spend some time in town and visit the Interagency Visitor Center for the Grand Staircase-Escalante National Monument.

From Escalante, drive southeast 4.6 miles on UT 12 to the signed Hole-in-the-Rock Road 200 at the boundary for the Grand Staircase-Escalante National Monument. The dirt road stretches to the horizon, paralleling the Kaiparowits Plateau, the setting for western writer Zane Grey's novel *Wild Horse Mesa.* According to Escalante locals, there is a tale about a golden statue of Jesus allegedly stolen from the Spanish and hidden on top of the Kaiparowits. Renowned scout and Mormon missionary Llewellyn Harris learned of the statue from a Navajo elder, who gave him a map drawn on a deerskin. Llewellyn Harris explored the plateau in 1888 and 1889, but returned emptyhanded.

During the 1940s and 1950s, a truck road was constructed that followed very closely the pioneer road. Whereas the modern road must zigzag to climb in and out of the gulches, the wagon road usually went straight down and up—much too steep for motorized four-wheel-drive vehicles. The original trail is marked with wooden posts with an outline of a covered wagon on them. Feel free to walk on the old trail, but please do not drive or mountain bike on it.

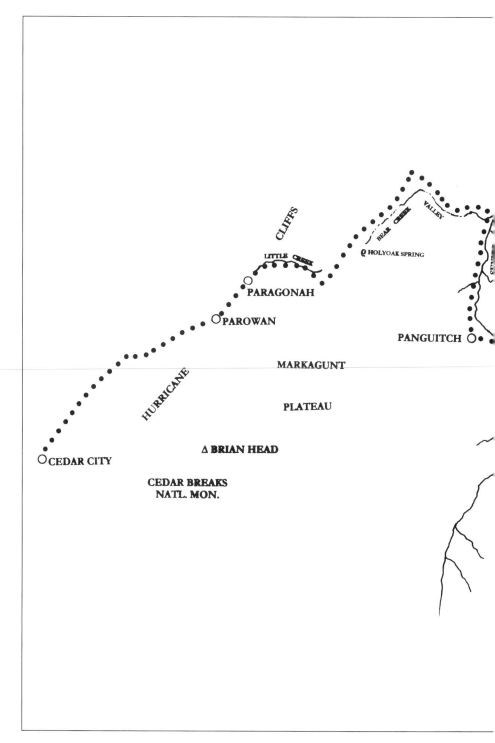

Map 2. HOLE-IN-THE-ROCK TRAIL, CEDAR CITY TO WIDTSOE JUNCTION.

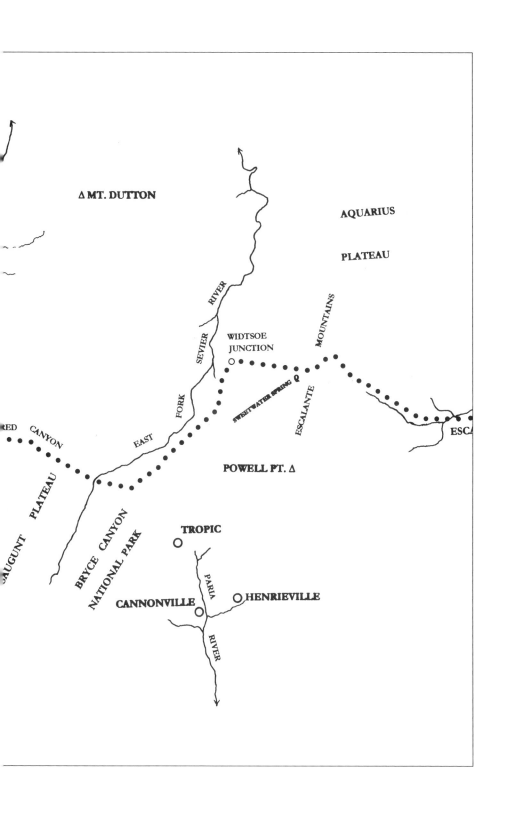

△ MT. DUTTON

AQUARIUS

PLATEAU

RIVER

SEVIER

WIDTSOE
JUNCTION

MOUNTAINS

SWEETWATER SPRING

ESCALANTE

FORK

RED   CANYON

EAST

ESC

POWELL PT. △

AUGUNT   PLATEAU

BRYCE   CANYON

NATIONAL   PARK

TROPIC

PARIA

CANNONVILLE

HENRIEVILLE

RIVER

The Hole-in-the-Rock Road is usually passable for any high-clearance vehicle at least as far as Dance Hall Rock. Beyond that point, the road becomes progressively worse. Also, note that storms may limit accessibility; check at the Escalante Interagency Visitor and Recreation Center. The road dead-ends at the Hole-in-the-Rock, overlooking Lake Powell, thus requiring driving back to Escalante.

Twelve miles down the Hole-in-the-Rock Road brings you to the short spur road (right) leading to the bizarre erosional features of Devil's Garden, certainly worth a visit. After driving another 2 miles on the Hole-in-the-Rock Road, you will come to Twentymile Wash.

It's another 23 miles to Dance Hall Rock, a National Historic Site. Take a stroll up and behind the rock to see some truly amazing potholes. Entire cottonwood trees are growing inside some of them. These are some of the largest potholes known on the Colorado Plateau. Erosion has carved them into the soft lower member of the Entrada Sandstone.

Not quite another mile beyond Dance Hall Rock is the turnoff (left) to the important Fortymile Spring camp area. Walk or drive in about a mile to the developed spring.

⚑5⚐

To the Brink

November 1879 to January 25, 1880

Considering all the time and toil spent in building a road through the Hole-in-the-Rock, it may be surprising that the pioneers never considered it an impassable barrier. It was the country on the east side of the Colorado River that gave them pause. Samuel Rowley remarked, "Before we left our homes we were told that the country had been explored, and that the road was feasible. But now we found that someone had been mistaken."

Would they have to turn back? William W. Hutchings, George B. Hobbs, Kumen Jones, and George Lewis were chosen by Jens Nielson to explore to the canyon rim, find a way down for wagons, locate a suitable river crossing, and explore for a way out of the Colorado River gorge to the east. After ten days, they returned to Fortymile Spring about the same time that President Smith arrived (November 27). They reported that there was no feasible route for a wagon road "in the draws of the Grand Canyon." (This gorge is, of course, Glen Canyon, not the Grand Canyon, which begins about eighty miles downstream in Arizona.) They had also encountered two prospectors who told them, "If every rag or other property owned by the people of the Territory were sold for cash, it would not pay for the making of a burro trail across the river."

Figure 11. THERE IS NO HINT OF THE HOLE-IN-THE-ROCK AND GLEN CANYON AS THE WAGON ROAD APPROACHES THE RIM. NAVAJO MOUNTAIN IS IN THE DISTANCE BEYOND BOTH GLEN CANYON AND THE SAN JUAN RIVER GORGE. THE STRAIGHT CLIFFS OF THE KAIPAROWITS PLATEAU ARE ON THE RIGHT.

The pioneers were trapped between the Kaiparowits Plateau and the maze of gulches draining into the Escalante River. Behind them, snows were deepening in the Escalante Mountains. Ahead was a 1,000-foot-deep canyon containing the 300-foot-wide river. Road construction halted.

But then Escalante residents Hall, Schow, and Collett arrived in camp, expressing their views that the scouts had simply missed the suitable crossing. They had also brought with them another small boat.

Another scouting party was sent out, accompanied by the three men from Escalante. The thirteen men examined the crack in the canyon rim that Platte D. Lyman called the Hole-in-the-Rock, then went about two miles upstream and lowered the boat to the river, which was "sluggish and the water milky but of good taste." They rowed down to the mouth of the Hole and camped. One of the "boys" caught a twelve-pound and a seven-pound "white salmon," which they had for breakfast and dinner.

(Today called Colorado pikeminnow, these now rare, endangered fish historically grew up to six feet in length, could weigh more than eighty pounds, and lived more than fifty years.)

They spent the next several days exploring along the river and to the east. In a side canyon, they caught "several mud turtles." (This is curious since the only modern record of turtles in the Glen Canyon region is the painted turtle, *Chrysemys picta.*) Even Platte D. Lyman was discouraged: "It is certainly the worst country I ever saw. . . . [M]ost of us are satisfied that there is no use of this company undertaking to get through to the San Juan this way."

In a cold rain on December 3, the scouts returned to camp and retired to President Smith's tent. Hobbs, Collett, and Schow were still optimistic about continuing through the maze of slickrock canyons. In particular, Collett and Schow claimed that they had only to climb a short distance from the east bank of the Colorado River to see the San Juan River. Unfortunately for the wagon train, they would discover that this was not true.

Jens Nielson said in his heavy Danish accent that if the saints had plenty of "stickie-ta-tudy" they could not fail, but the final decision should be left to "the president and the Lord." Although President Smith had not yet seen the Hole or the country beyond, after listening to all of the reports, positive and negative, he believed that continuing was the course to take. The next day he called a meeting of the whole camp to get everyone's sentiments. Few, if any, of the colonists dissented. They were unified as never before; they would go on. They broke out in song: "The spirit of God like a fire is burning." Road construction resumed.

The territorial legislature was about to convene in Salt Lake City, and Smith, a prominent past member, agreed to petition the lawmakers to acquire more blasting powder, additional tools, and other supplies for the party. Smith thought he would be gone only several weeks at most, but while in Salt Lake he became deathly ill and did not return to the

Figure 12. AN AERIAL VIEW LOOKING STRAIGHT DOWN THE HOLE-IN-THE-ROCK.

mission until the next spring. Fortunately, the needed supplies arrived, and by default Platte D. Lyman was appointed field captain.

About December 16, work began on the Hole. Lyman surveyed the crack that was initially too narrow to allow passage for even a man, let alone a wagon. He found that the road gradient would have to drop 8 vertical feet for each horizontal rod (16.5 feet) for the first third of the distance to the river, and 5.5 feet to the rod for the rest.

Nielson and the Perkins brothers, Benjamin and Hyrum, were in charge of blasting the notch. The Perkins, "the blasters and blowers from Wales," had had experience in coal mines in the British Isles. During the first few days of work, men were either lowered over the edge on ropes or walked a couple miles upstream, descended to the river, and approached the Hole from below. Picks, shovels, sledgehammers, and chisels made the rock fly, and the existing 45-foot-deep crack was widened and deepened to allow the passage of wagons.

At the base of the crack, the road builders had to avoid a sheer drop. Ben Perkins designed a way to hang a road on the cliff face. First, a

Figure 13. UNCLE BEN'S DUGWAY. WOODEN STAKES
WERE POUNDED INTO THE DRILL HOLES A FEW FEET
BELOW THE ROCK SHELF TO SUPPORT THIS SECTION OF
THE TRAIL.

50-foot-long shelf was cut out of the sandstone for the inside wagon
wheels to follow. Some 5 feet below and parallel to the shelf, holes were
drilled out to accept wooden stakes. The cliff was so steep that the work-
ers had to be held in place with ropes. Then more logs, brush, and dirt
were piled on top of the wooden stakes to build up a road for the outside
wheels. Uncle Ben's Dugway was an engineering feat to behold.

The precipitous gradient of the Hole then eased up and graded into
a steep but sandy slope. Across the Colorado River, another dugway had
to be constructed up a 250-foot solid sandstone wall.

Figure 14. The wagon trail can be seen approaching the rim of Glen Canyon at the Hole-in-the-Rock. Boats now race across Lake Powell where pioneer wagons had to be ferried across the mighty Colorado River.

The two blacksmiths in the party were among the most important men on the trip. One was non-Mormon Wilson Dailey, who had joined the group to reach the mines in Colorado; the other was George Lewis. The smiths not only kept horses and oxen shod but were also kept busy sharpening and repairing tools.

During the first week of January, Charles Hall and two sons arrived at the Hole with the lumber for a ferry. Hall had had the lumber cut to his specifications in Escalante. The lumber was hand carried down the Hole to the river and the raft assembled. A kiln for pitch was constructed

Figure 15. THE WAGON TRAIL DROPS OFF GREY MESA INTO A MAZE OF SLICKROCK HILLS AND HOLLOWS.

right on the riverbank so caulking would be readily available. By the time the wagon road was completed, a ferry capable of carrying two wagons at a time was waiting.

~ THE FOUR SCOUTS: DECEMBER 17 TO JANUARY 9 ~

While the road was being built to reach the Colorado River, four men were sent out to scout the country east of the river: George B. Hobbs, who had been on the earlier exploratory trip to the San Juan, George W. Sevy, Lemuel H. Redd Sr., and George Morrell. They took two pack animals and two riding mounts. According to their calculations, it was only seventy miles to Montezuma Fort in a straight line. Not wanting to be overburdened, they packed only eight days' worth of rations, figuring that they could easily cover twenty miles a day.

After crossing the Colorado, they climbed out of the river gorge and traveled over to Grey Mesa, where they encountered "14 llamas" (most likely desert bighorn sheep). (This is another curious animal sighting in that Hobbs surely knew the difference between llamas and sheep. Besides, llamas, South American natives, would not have been in the wilds of southeastern Utah in the nineteenth century.) Hobbs followed one of the sheep off the mesa, which turned out to be the only possible route down the precipitous "Slick Rocks" to the desert below.

They continued northeasterly, passing Lake Pagahrit (Hermit Lake) and eventually dropping into Castle Wash to Green Water Spring. Here three canyons coalesced. They explored each one; two boxed up, but one did not. Continuing up that one, they stumbled upon a cliff dwelling (Castle Ruin) with seven rooms and a bake oven that Hobbs claimed was in serviceable condition. Farther along was a fork. Hobbs explored the more easterly branch while the others went up the other, where they encountered a bear. Hobbs came upon "the old Cliff Dweller trail again" that led them up and over Clay Hills Pass. (Unfortunately, we don't have a better description of this and other "old Indian trails" that these pioneers stumbled upon. Archaeologists today are discovering that some of the prehistoric trails were actually constructed, and some are quite remarkable in scale and unwavering straightness.)

Once over the pass, they headed around steep-walled Grand Gulch and camped about three miles west of Cow Tank. The next evening found them at Dripping Spring and the following day at Grand Flat, their seventh day out (December 23). Eight inches of snow fell during the night, making it hard to find their animals in the morning. That night they cooked a "slapjack," or a large pancake, the last of their food.

The rugged terrain around the head of Grand Gulch forced them up onto the side of Elk Ridge on Christmas Day, without food and not a recognizable landmark in sight. Desperate, Hobbs climbed a small hill (Salvation or Christmas Knoll), where he spied the Blue Mountains (Abajos). They could now locate themselves and resume their journey to Montezuma Fort. The next day they dropped into Comb Wash at the

Figure 16. THE MODERN HIGHWAY, U.S. 163, HAS BEEN BLASTED THROUGH COMB RIDGE WHERE GEORGE HOBBS AND THE OTHER THREE SCOUTS FOLLOWED AN ANCIENT INDIAN TRAIL.

base of Comb Ridge, but it wasn't until the following day that they found a trail going through a break in the thousand-foot cliff.

After climbing up and over Comb Ridge, they encountered yet another major gulch: Butler Wash. This was their third night out without food. Hobbs, unsure if he would survive, carved his name and "Jan 1." (When he was recounting the event thirty-seven years later, he may have been confused, the actual date probably being December 27 or else he inscribed the date on his return journey.) Snow fell during the night, and a band of Navajos passed nearby. The scouts finally found a way across and took turns riding the animals.

As they approached where Bluff is now, they saw a calf and thought about eating it but realized that help must be near. Indeed, in a little while they came to a camp of white people, ten adults and five children, from Colorado, who had settled there in August. Supper was offered and readily accepted. The famished explorers gorged on fresh-baked biscuits and roasted meat.

The next day, the four scouts made their way to Montezuma Fort. As they were crossing Montezuma Creek, they met Ernest Mitchell and James Merrick (given as Merritt or Merick in some accounts). The two men said that they were looking for an isolated spot for a cattle ranch. The scouts mentioned Lake Pagahrit and suggested that Mitchell and Merrick wait for them. At the fort, the scouts found the Harrimans, the Davises, and Harvey Dunton surviving on ground seed wheat and a little meat.

Where to get supplies for the return trip was a major problem. Providence shined down on them when a trapper (possibly Peter Shirts) happened by, and they were able to buy forty-eight pounds of flour from him. The families at the fort thought they could hold out for sixty more days. The scouts promised to send help within that time. (Hobbs did return on February 24 with supplies.)

On the last day of 1879, the four scouts plus Dunton started on their return trip. After crossing Montezuma Creek, they again encountered Mitchell and Merrick and learned of their true quest. The two men believed the Navajos had a secret silver mine and were going in search of it. They wanted Hobbs to join them, but he refused. The scouts and two prospectors parted company at Comb Wash—which was fortuitous, since the bodies of Mitchell and Merrick were discovered in Monument Valley the next February.

The scouts found a different old trail leading west, which helped them travel faster, but then Dan Harris caught up to them and insisted that he knew a better way. Instead, the six of them got tangled up in the convoluted country around Grand Gulch. A snowstorm further hampered their travel. But they eventually reached Clay Hills Pass, discovering a spring along the way. They had been living on one pound of flour a day, but now it was all gone. They retraced their trail down Castle Wash toward Lake Pagahrit. Snow covered the ground, hampering their progress. When they reached Slick Rocks, they had trouble scaling the icy five hundred-foot hill, but once on top of Grey Mesa, their pace quickened. Twenty-four days after starting out from the Hole, the scouting party, emaciated but alive, finally arrived back at the Colorado River on January 9.

—◆◆◆◆◆—

Between Fortymile Spring and the Hole, the country gets more and more convoluted. What looks like a flat, level plain hides numerous deep gulches. The pioneers either had to find a way down and out of each one or attempt to skirt around each canyon by going closer to the base of the Straight Cliffs.

In early December, about half of the company was camped at Fiftymile Spring, and the other half camped near the top of the Hole. The latter group had to melt snow or find water caught in natural rock tanks. Those camped at Fiftymile Spring were responsible for building the road out of the Colorado River gorge, while the others were blasting and filling the crack so wagons could be driven to the river. The "fifty-milers" walked to their construction site on Monday mornings, crossed the river, worked all week, and returned Saturday evening.

Firewood was scarce. The abundant shadscale was good for only the smallest fires, so wood was hauled from distant woodlands. Food was also beginning to run short. Seed wheat and other grains were ground in small coffee mills to provide flour for bread making. Parched corn became a regular part of the pioneers' diet. Some food, like beans, corn, and sorghum, came in from Escalante, but pretty soon most of them were eating just bread and beef.

Forage was also very limited around the Hole-in-the-Rock, so some of the men attempted to drive horses down to Jackass Bench, but nine of the animals slipped on the barren sandstone, justifiably called slickrock, and fell to their deaths. Platte D. Lyman reported, "Found one of my mules in a ditch and so weak that it could not stand so I killed it."

As the days grew shorter, cold, snowy weather prevailed. Mrs. Henry James Riley carried her baby with his little feet in the front of her dress against her body to keep them from freezing.

Despite their isolated camp, as Christmas approached, the children were certain that Santa would find them. So on Christmas Eve, they tied stockings to wagon wheels and sang carols before going to bed. The next morning, they discovered parched corn and cookies in their stockings.

During Christmas Day, the adults danced and sang in celebration and held a shooting contest to win select cuts of beef. They did not know that the four scouts were lost in a blizzard east of the Colorado River, desperately trying to survive.

At Fiftymile Spring on January 3, the James B. Decker wagon box was lifted off the running gears and placed on the ground. Snow was banked around the box to keep out drafts. With Ellen Hobbs Fielding assisting, James's wife, Anna Maria, gave birth to Lena Deseret.

Three weeks later on the evening of January 25, after eight weeks of hard labor, the road crew announced that the road through the Hole-in-the-Rock was ready.

⊕ Following the Trail ⊕

From the Fortymile Spring turnoff to the Hole-in-the-Rock, the scenery becomes more dramatic, and an increasing number of gulches force the road to go closer to the base of the Straight Cliffs. In about 9 miles, the road enters the Glen Canyon National Recreation Area.

Beyond this point, the last 10 miles of road to the rim of Glen Canyon and the Hole begin to deteriorate into a very rough four-wheel-drive track.

The exact location of the Fiftymile Spring camp is in doubt. On the modern topographic map, it could be Soda Spring in Soda Gulch (where there are some remnants of dugouts up the gulch) or about a mile south at the Bailey ranch cabin, labeled Fiftymile Spring. Another mile southeast is yet another spring. In all likelihood, the pioneers utilized all three.

Not far from the pioneers' Fiftymile Spring camp, twenty-year-old enigmatic artist, vagabond, and lover of wild places Everett Ruess disappeared in 1934. Searchers found the word NEMO scratched under an arch... Greek for "no one." Is this a land where no one belongs? Nemo is also the name of the submarine captain from the Jules Verne novel *Twenty Thousand Leagues under the Sea,* which Ruess was reading. Did Ruess envision himself a wanderer in the canyons "under" the earth? What was Ruess's fate?

At the Hole itself, it's possible to clamber down to Lake Powell. Although published accounts state the vertical drop from the canyon rim to the Colorado River to be up to 2,000 feet, a check of the topographic map shows that it is closer to 1,200 feet—still a formidable drop for a wagon. The pioneer road's grade averaged 25 percent with several 45 percent pitches. At full pool, Lake Powell is about 500 feet deep at the Hole, so the upper 700 feet, the most spectacular portion of the road, is never covered by water.

At the top of the Hole, on the right-hand side, one can find the only remaining inscription of the San Juan Mission pioneers west of the Colorado River. It reads simply: "Decker, 1880." There were five separate Decker families in the party. Pieces of Uncle Ben's Dugway, including the sandstone shelf and the holes drilled for the log supports, can be seen.

About 18 miles as the raven flies northeast of the Hole, Charles Hall located an easier Colorado River crossing and established a ferry there in 1881, which was abandoned after major flooding in 1884. But the Hole continued to see some use. In late 1899, members of the Hoskaninni Company, the largest gold mining company ever to operate along the Colorado River, carved large steps down the Hole. Engineer, Colorado River explorer, and head of the company Robert B. Stanton sent a party of twenty-six men under Nathaniel Galloway to improve the pioneer road through the Hole for pack stock. The large steps carved into the upper part of the Hole were done at this time. This was going to be a major gateway into Glen Canyon. Separating the fine flour gold from the

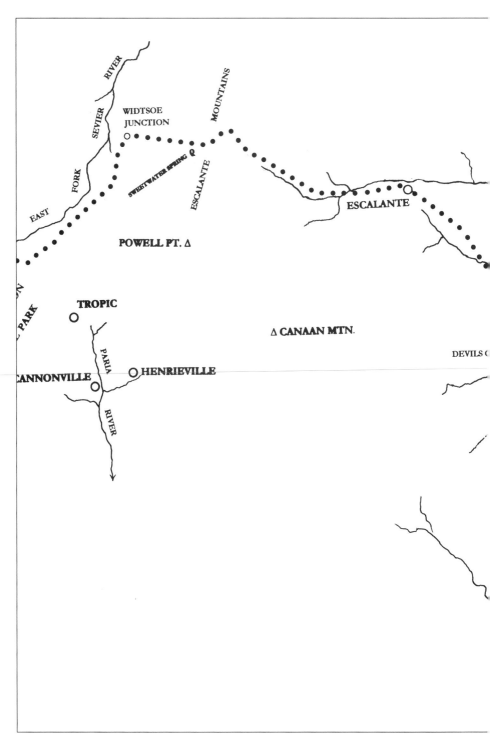

Map 3. Hole–in–the–Rock Trail, Widtsoe Junction to Hole–in–the–Rock.

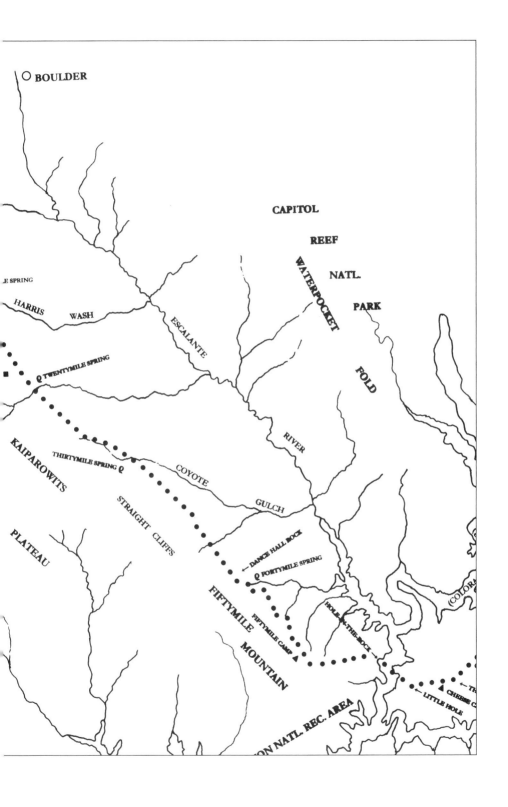

O BOULDER

CAPITOL

REEF

WATERPOCKET

NATL.

PARK

FOLD

.E SPRING

HARRIS   WASH

ESCALANTE

Q TWENTYMILE SPRING

KAIPAROWITS

THIRTYMILE SPRING Q

COYOTE

RIVER

STRAIGHT CLIFFS

GULCH

PLATEAU

DANCE HALL ROCK

Q FORTYMILE SPRING

FIFTYMILE

FIFTYMILE CAMP

HOLE IN-THE-ROCK

(COLORA

MOUNTAIN

TH

LITTLE HOLE

CHEESE C

ON NATL. REC. AREA

Figure 17. HOLE-IN-THE-ROCK AND MEMBERS OF THE HOSKANINNI MINING COMPANY IN 1898. COURTESY OF DWIGHT L. SMITH.

river mud proved uneconomical, and the Hoskaninni Company pulled out in 1901.

Navajos, Paiutes, and Utes were quick to use the old trail to reach settlements west of the river and to hunt on the Kaiparowits Plateau. Henry N. Cowles and Joseph T. Hall (no relation to Charles Hall) decided to build a trading post at the base of the Hole in 1900 to take advantage of the traffic. For about two years, they carried on a lively business, exchanging foodstuffs, tobacco, yardage, and hardware for hides, wools, and textiles.

When legendary geologist Herbert Gregory saw the Hole in the early 1900s, he was so incredulous that he believed the pioneer wagons had to be disassembled and carried down this part of the trail. Over time, much of the pioneer fill material at the Hole has washed away, and large boulders have tumbled in.

From Escalante to the Hole is at minimum 123 miles round-trip, not counting any side trips. There is no gas or reliable water nor any other facilities except in Escalante. Go prepared.

After retracing your route back to UT 12 Scenic Byway, turn right (northeast) to Boulder. The next 20 miles is some of the most spectacular paved driving in the world. In town, the Anasazi Indian State Park describes the prehistoric Indian life of the area.

From "downtown" Boulder, follow the paved 29-mile Burr Trail Scenic Backway to spectacular Capitol Reef National Park. The next 7 miles of gravel switchbacks passing through the park are sometimes rough, but as you leave the park to continue toward Bullfrog Marina, the road improves and is paved again after another 11 miles. It's another 24 miles to the marina.

The John Atlantic Burr Ferry connects Bullfrog with Hall's Crossing Marina. For the ferry schedule, check http://www.lakepowell.com or call 435.684.7000 or 435.684.3000.

Of course, another way to reach the Hole-in-the-Rock is by boat. The Hole is at buoy M66, about 66 miles up the lake from Wahweap Marina or about 28 miles down the lake from Hall's Crossing Marina.

6

Down the Hole and Beyond

January 26 to April 1880

To look down the Hole gives one pause. Who drove the first wagon down through the Hole is a title claimed by several folks but in truth is forgotten. Platte D. Lyman, who kept a journal during the trip, did not record this fact. It doesn't really matter since each descent turned into a personal adventure.

The hind wagon wheels were "rough-locked." A heavy chain was wrapped around the felloe rim and iron tire of the wheel, with the loose end fastened to the wagon box or running gears so that the wrapped part of the wheel would be at the bottom. The two locked wheels could not turn but would dig into the ground. Freighters had come up with this method for going down steep descents.

The locked wheels on the first few outfits going down mired into the loose sand and gravel and pushed an avalanche of material. As the day progressed, there was less and less sand and gravel to slow the wagons. Long ropes or chains were attached to the rear axle so that men could hang on behind to help slow the wagon. Sometimes a horse or mule was used in the same manner, but this didn't work well. Some of the animals were thrown to the ground and dragged down the steep grade. Danielson B. Barney tied two large cedar trees to his wagon to act as brakes.

At the end of the day, Joseph Stanford Smith, who had been helping with getting the wagons on the ferry, discovered that his wagon was still at the top with his wife, Arabella, and small children. Many years later, his grandchildren related that he hesitated about even trying the descent, but Belle, as she was known, encouraged her husband: "I'll do the holding back on old Nig's lines. Isn't that what he's tied back there for?"

"But, Belle, the children?"

Back a ways from the crevice, she set three-year-old Roy on a folded quilt and put the baby between his legs. "Hold little brother 'til Papa comes for you." She had Ada sit in front of her brothers.

Ada turned toward her father, "Will you come back, Papa?" He could only nod yes while trying to hold back the tears. "Then I'm not afraid. We'll stay here with God 'til you and Mama get the wagon down."

The wagon eased into the narrow crack then lurched downward. Old Nig was thrown to his haunches. Belle managed to keep her balance for a little longer but then went sprawling. The wagon hit a huge boulder, and the impact jerked Belle back to her feet but flung her against the cliff. The wagon stopped with the team wedged under the tongue. Smith jumped down to loosen the harness and free the team. He looked up and saw Belle, her face white against the red sandstone but defiant, blood-smeared, dirt-begrimed, and eyes flashing. A trickle of blood ran down her leg.

"Is your leg broken?"

She wouldn't have his sympathy, not just yet anyway. "Does that feel like it's broken?" she said as she kicked him in the shin. Smith quickly climbed back to the rim and retrieved the children.

Amazingly, in spite of the steepness and difficulty, all the wagons from the Hole Camp, about forty-one of the eighty-three in the total train, made it to the river, and most were ferried across that day, including Joseph Smith's. Two wagons could fit on the raft, while most of the cattle and horses swam across. George W. Decker reckoned that he forded the Colorado at least twenty times while herding livestock across.

During one of the river crossings, the ferry was nearly lost when a sudden gust of wind swept the raft downstream and brought it dangerously close to some rapids. Most of the crossings went without incident, but an unruly ox knocked poor Alfred A. Barney in. Fortunately, Barney managed to swim to shore. His father remarked, "I didn't know the boy could swim."

Before the remainder of the wagons, about forty-two more, got across, colder weather set in. Shore ice extended several feet out into the river, making the operation more complicated, but all the wagons reached the east shore. Then the river froze over completely, and many otters and beaver emerged and played on the ice.

Short dugways led from the river up to a bench between two cliffs, where more than a dozen pioneers chiseled their names (Register Rocks). Then the road dropped into Cottonwood Canyon. It was relatively easy going along a little, clear meandering stream. About three miles up Cottonwood, the vanguard of the expedition established a camp in a grove of cottonwoods on January 30. A second camp was made about a half mile downstream. There was plenty of forage and firewood and an abundance of clean water. The women did a major wash, the first since leaving Escalante three months prior.

The Cottonwood camps lasted about ten days while the men went out and literally carved a road through the solid sandstone ahead. The first obstacle was the climb out of Cottonwood Canyon—Cottonwood Hill. The first part was through fine drifting sand. Next a dugway was blasted up a sandstone butte, the only place to put a road in this convoluted landscape. The road continued up and through a V-shaped notch, named Little Hole-in-the-Rock, to the top of Little Mesa. From there the road meandered a mile or so to their next camp.

Cottonwood Hill was so steep that seven teams of horses or as many yokes of oxen were required to pull each wagon to the top. The first wagons started out on February 10. Several wagons tipped over, but luckily no one was injured. A hive of bees was dumped out of one wagon, but they were so cold that they were easily sacked up. Another wagon upset with a child inside. Fortunately, she was wrapped up in a feather bed so she wasn't injured, but all the dishes were broken.

At the next camp, two men from the Panguitch Tithing Office arrived with two hundred pounds of pork and forty pounds of cheese. Since the cheese wouldn't go far feeding 236 people, it was decided to auction it off, the money going back to the settlements to purchase more supplies. After that, this place became known as Cheese Camp.

While at Cheese Camp, some of the members who were driving large herds of horses wanted to go ahead of the rest. This didn't sit well with some pioneers, since they didn't want the horses eating everything before the other teams and oxen could continue. The situation almost escalated into violence, but a compromise was reached when the horsemen declared that they would drive as quickly as possible across Grey Mesa and beyond so forage would be available for everyone.

From Cheese Camp, the road had to be cut again in solid rock up a small, dry canyon, then over and around ledges, before dipping into the upper reaches of Wilson Canyon and out a very narrow crack or chute. Although the Chute was barely wide enough for the wagons, at least there was no danger of tipping over.

From the top of the Chute, the route followed along a rocky ridge for about two miles to the base of Grey Mesa, which forms the backbone between the Colorado and San Juan drainages. Elizabeth Decker sighed, "It's the roughest country you or anybody else ever seen; it's nothing in the world but rocks and holes, hills and hollows. The mountains are just one solid rock as smooth as an apple."

By contrast, Grey Mesa was seven miles of flat, sandy tableland fifteen hundred feet above the rivers. And though the shadscale, blackbrush, and grass were covered by a foot of snow, it was some of the best forage their animals had had in a while. To the north, snow blanketed the rugged Henry Mountains; to the south loomed the rounded dome of Navajo Mountain; the long, flat top of the Kaiparowits Plateau made up

Figure 18. Skidding ATV tires have marked the wagon trail going up the Chute.

the western horizon; and to the east, the gentle rise of Nokai Dome blocked the view.

A howling blizzard was raging when another baby decided it was time to be born. Mons and Olivia Larson were on their way to a new home in Arizona when they heard about the San Juan expedition and thought traveling with it would be shorter and easier than via Lee's Ferry. But now it was February 21, and the baby was ready to come out.

While Mons was trying to pitch their tent, John Rio, so-named because they were perched on Grey Mesa above the San Juan River, was

Figure 19. THIS IS PART OF THE ORIGINAL WAGON TRAIL ATOP GREY MESA ABOUT WHERE JOHN RIO LARSON WAS BORN DURING A RAGING BLIZZARD ON FEBRUARY 21, 1880.

born while his mother was lying on the spring seat out in the wind. After only four days, he and his mother were ready to travel. If it wasn't snowing, Olivia would bathe him; otherwise, she would just rub his little body down with flannel. At the far northeastern end of Grey Mesa, where the bighorn sheep had led George Hobbs down the steep five hundred-foot drop, it took the road builders a cold, windy, miserable week to carve out one-half mile of dugways to get the wagons down.

From Slick Rocks, the trail ran northeast seven miles across Death Valley to the east side of Table Top Mesa and on to a lovely, clear J-shaped lake, some fifty feet deep, a half mile long, and a quarter mile wide. Drifting sand had dammed up a canyon, and a little stream filled up this reservoir, which became variously known as Lake Pagahrit and Hermit Lake. To cross the canyon the wagons were driven across the top of the sand dam. Platte D. Lyman noted: "Cottonwood, willow, canes, flags, bulrushes and several kinds of grass grow luxuriantly.... On a

Figure 20. LOOKING DOWN THE SLICK ROCKS PORTION OF THE WAGON TRAIL OFF GREY MESA. THE HENRY MOUNTAINS ARE IN THE DISTANCE.

point of rock jutting into the lake are the remains of an old stone fortification built probably several hundred years ago."

While some did housekeeping chores at the lake, the road builders completed a road up Castle Wash to Clay Hills Pass. Though the sand was deep in places, the going was relatively easy, the weather generally mild, and Green Spring and Irish Green Spring supplied plenty of water for man and beast.

Near the Castle Ruin cliff dwelling, "E. L. Lyman," "J. Smith" (there were three J. Smiths in the party), and "March 5, 1880" were carved into the soft Navajo sandstone. Three miles farther east, "S. S. Smith, March 10, 1880" was inscribed, presumably by S. S. Smith Jr. since the senior Smith was still in Salt Lake City.

By March 5, wagons were gathering on top of Clay Hills Pass looking down to the desert floor below. Another week of road building was required to construct the three miles of road necessary to descend the thousand vertical feet of sticky blue clay. Someone inscribed on a boulder near the top of the pass: "Make Peace With God."

While the road building was going on, Lyman and several others explored ahead to mark the way and also made a side trip across Whirlwind Bench down to Clay Hills Crossing on the San Juan River, where they found about two hundred acres of flat potential farmland timbered with cottonwood trees.

On March 13 the road down from the pass was completed, but as wagons began to roll another major blizzard struck. The camp at the bottom of the pass was buried in snow. Wagon covers were ripped by the winds, and tents tipped over. The temperature plummeted. Lyman confided, "Last night was the coldest night I ever experienced, it was impossible to be comfortable in bed or anywhere else."

To circumvent the maze of canyons around Grand Gulch, their road had to go fairly close to the base of Red House Cliffs, passing Red House Spring, Cow Tank, and Dripping Spring along the way to near the base of Elk Ridge.

The road conditions varied with the weather. Sometimes there were up to two feet of snow and other times bottomless mud. The animals were worn out. Some folks hitched an ox and a mule together. Some were using heifers and cows as teams. The wagon train was spread out over thirty miles. A few wagons were abandoned to be picked up later.

It was along this part of the trail that an old Ute Indian rode into camp. He had never seen a wagon in these parts and excitedly wanted to know where they had come from and where they were going. When informed about their route, he threw his arms up in disbelief.

Figure 21. Horizontal grooves were carved into the sandstone to help the wagons descend Slick Rocks on Grey Mesa.

As the train neared the base of Elk Ridge, the pinyon pine—juniper woodland of Cedar Mesa grew more and more dense, which required a crew of choppers to go out and clear a path through the trees. Whenever they reached a natural clearing or flat, they gave it a name. Thus Harmony Flat, Grand Flat, Mormon Flat, Long Flat, and Snow Flat (where the snow line was) were christened.

By late March, they emerged from the woodland while dropping a couple of thousand feet off Cedar Mesa into Comb Wash. To their im-

Figure 22. The treacherous bentonite clays on the east side of Clay Hills Pass.

mediate east rose the impenetrable wall of Comb Ridge, a thousand-foot-high escarpment that runs from Elk Ridge southward across the San Juan River down into Arizona. Although an old Indian trail cut through the cliff at Navajo Hill (Navajo Spring), that trail was suitable only for foot traffic, not wagons.

The wagons rumbled down the wash for about ten miles, where they finally reached the banks of the San Juan River. The pioneers hoped to travel along its north bank to Montezuma Fort. But this was not to be. The river was in spring flood, and there was no room for a road.

✦ Following the Trail ✦

The section of the Hole-in-the-Rock Trail from Lake Powell to UT 276, Hall's Crossing Road, is the least accessible but in many respects the most incredible part of the pioneers' entire route. To approach this section by land requires a stout and dependable four-wheel-drive vehicle,

FIGURE 23. GRAND GULCH WAS ONLY ONE OF MANY DEEP
CANYONS INCISED INTO CEDAR MESA THAT HAD TO BE
BYPASSED BY THE WAGON TRAIN.

an ATV of some kind, hiking boots, or a sturdy trail horse and good
map-reading skills.

In 1940, Lynn Lyman, son of original pioneer Walter C. Lyman, led
the first party of descendants to retrace the Hole-in-the-Rock Trail.
Eighty-two people and 143 pack and riding animals took part. Two with
the original party also participated: Caroline Redd, who was six years old
in 1879-1880, and Charlie Walton, who was ten years old. Legendary

river runner Norman Nevills was on hand to ferry people across the Colorado. He made eighteen round-trips, taking five passengers at a time.

From Hall's Crossing Marina, follow UT 276 east for about 14 miles, just short of milepost 59, then turn right (south) onto dirt County Road 2131. Look to the left in about 0.3 mile for an old drill-hole pipe next to a wash. The original trail crossed the road and continued up the wash. About 2 miles from UT 276, you come to an intersection. Turn right (southwest), still on County Road 2131. In about 4 miles, notice an abandoned half-track truck. Turn right (northwest) here onto County Road 2511, which is where four-wheel-drive becomes necessary. After 3.6 miles, another intersection is reached. (This road to the right is an alternate route from UT 276. It leaves the pavement immediately west of the Calvin Black Airport and reaches this juncture in about 4 miles.) Turn left (southwest), and in about 2.2 miles the rim of the East Fork of Lake Canyon is reached.

Perched on the edge of the East Fork are low walls of limestone blocks. This large prehistoric ruin was occupied roughly from A.D. 1150 to 1300. Pottery evidence indicates an affiliation with the Kayenta (northeastern Arizona) and Mesa Verde (southwestern Colorado) Anasazi, typical of this part of southeastern Utah.

However, this is not where the pioneers crossed Lake Canyon. The natural sand dam was located about a mile downstream. In 1915, cattleman J. A. Scorup witnessed the flood that topped the sand dam and cut a channel, which led to the draining of Lake Pagahrit, Paiute for "standing water." Continuing erosion has washed away most of the dam, which was located about a mile downstream. It is possible to drive down the steep slope and across the bottom of the East Fork of Lake Canyon, but only an ATV, hikers, or horseback riders will be able to ascend out the other side. From Lake Canyon to Lake Powell is about 23 miles of very technical off-road driving or moderate hiking; the last 3 miles from the top of Cottonwood Hill to Lake Powell has been closed to all vehicles since 1972. (When Lake Powell is full, the distance from Cottonwood Hill to

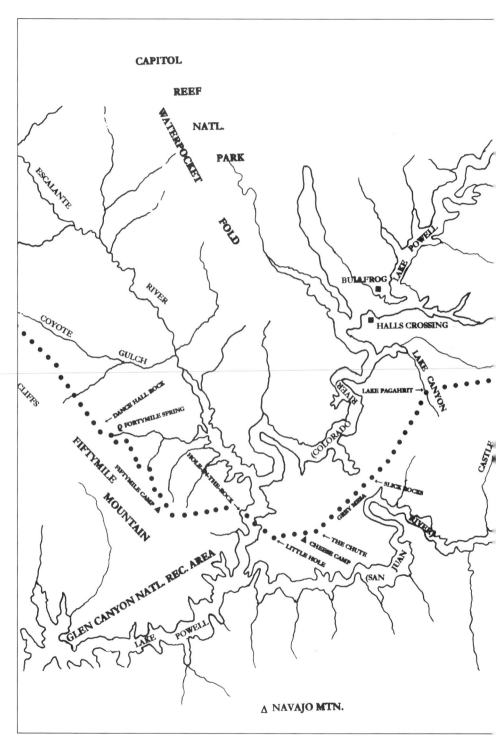

Map 4. Hole-in-the-Rock Trail, Hole-in-the-Rock to Grand Flat.

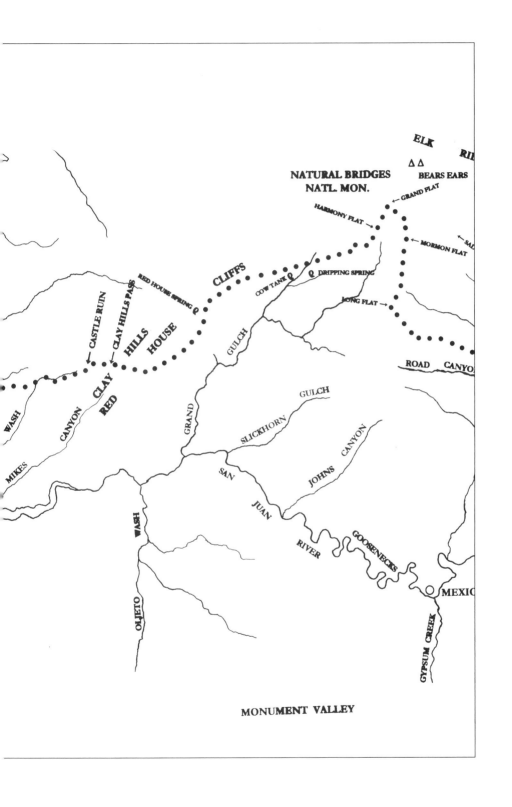

the lake is only about 1.5 miles.) The road is vague in places, especially where it crosses slickrock. For GPS waypoints of this section of trail, go online to http://www.4x4now.com/ppmay96.htm.

At the northeastern end of Grey Mesa, from the bottom of Iceberg Canyon, the modern road ascends the mesa a little west of the wagon route. The wagon route begins at a BLM sign about Grey Mesa. The steep steplike trail is unbelievable. It may be hard to follow higher up. But there are a few rock cairns, and the top of the wagon route is marked by a large vertical wooden stake on the skyline. Once on top of the mesa, Navajo Mountain and the Henry Mountains can be seen, both unusual in their origins. They are laccoliths or in a sense volcanoes that didn't quite make it. Magma working its way up to the surface pushed overlying sedimentary rock layers into mountains, but the molten rock never broke through to create a volcano or lava flow. Over millions of years, the overlying rocks have been eroded to expose the igneous cores. Farther east, the Abajos are another laccolithic range.

Edward Lyman and his son Kay, descendants of Platte Lyman, purchased a war-surplus Dodge weapons carrier and managed to drive it in April 1954 from Nokai Dome to just beyond Lake Canyon. The following month, three Willys Jeeps made it to the base of Grey Mesa. Over the next several years, uranium prospectors built other roads in the area, and on April 23, 1959, the first Jeeps made it all the way to the east bank of the Colorado River.

Perhaps the easiest way to approach the astonishing dugway, Little Hole-in-the-Rock, and the Chute is by boat. The mouth of Cottonwood Canyon is near buoy M63A. At high pool, Lake Powell inundates much of Cottonwood Canyon, including the lower portion of Register Rocks. However, the lake does not reach the main pioneer campsite near the head of Cottonwood Canyon. The hike from the lake to the dugway and Little Hole-in-the-Rock is about 3.5 miles and the Chute another 4 miles one way. About halfway between the Little Hole and the Chute, there is a relatively large flat area marked with another wooden pole, which is the site of Cheese Camp.

Back at UT 276, the modern highway closely follows the original wagon road to Clay Hills Pass. At milepost 68 on the north side of the highway is Castle Ruin (Hobbs's "Cliff Dwellers' dwelling") tucked into a sandstone alcove. Another mile and Irish Green Spring is reached; today it is the site of several trailers and corrals used by local ranchers. In 2 more miles, just east of the crest of Clay Hills Pass, is a scenic turnout and monument to the pioneers.

After bulldozing a new road over the pass in 1951, the Skelly Oil Company declared, "Clay Hill has been conquered." However, the unstable and malleable bentonite clays of the Chinle Formation continue to challenge road builders. Skelly drilled on Nokai Dome, east of Grey Mesa, but it was a dry hole. Today, it takes a discerning eye to locate the pioneer trail in the pass area. Many portions are too steep for any kind of ordinary four-wheel-drive vehicle.

From the pass turnout, continue east. Near the base of the hill, County Road 278 goes off to the right (south) 12 miles to Clay Hills Crossing. About 12.8 miles from the pass turnout, keep a sharp eye out for County Road 2301 (just west of milepost 86), which requires four-wheel-drive, possibly an ATV. Turn right (southeast) and drive 9.1 miles to where the road returns to pavement on UT 95.

Turn right (east), drive 6.1 miles, and then turn right (south) on UT 261. The pioneer trail takes a slight shortcut from Grand Flat to Mormon Flat, which can be walked.

Along UT 95 is the turnoff to Natural Bridges National Monument. These three extraordinary stone bridges are in nearby White Canyon.

To see Salvation Knoll, continue east on UT 95 another 4.2 miles. On the right (south) side of the highway at the base of the hill is an interpretive sign.

In about 5.1 miles on UT 261, the emigrants' trail angles southeast from Long Flat. However, this is a very rough track, County Road 253, so stay on UT 261 another 5.2 miles and then turn left (east) onto Snow Flat Road, County Road 237. This better dirt road, usually passable with just a high-clearance vehicle, joins the trail again in 4.5 miles.

From Snow Flat down to Comb Wash, you drive mostly on original road. Comb Ridge, a thousand-foot cliff that is the result of a monocline or gentle fold in the earth's crust, comes into view. As the dirt road descends off Cedar Mesa into Comb Wash, it makes a couple of tight switchbacks called "The Twist" on the USGS topographic map. The original pioneer trail was more direct. Continue south down Comb Wash to U.S. 163. The distance from UT 261 to U.S. 163 is about 25 miles.

The modern highway, U.S. 163, cuts through Comb Ridge at a spot called Navajo Hill, which was the location of the Indian trail that Hobbs and the other three scouts used.

Occasionally, there are guided excursions along the Hole-in-the-Rock Trail between Lake Powell and Bluff. Contact the Monticello Field Office of the Bureau of Land Management or the Hole-in-the-Rock Foundation for information.

☀7☀

"We Thank Thee"

March 28 to April 6, 1880

Upon reaching the San Juan River, the colonists were sure their travails were over. The river had done an excellent job of cutting a passage through Comb Ridge but didn't provide a continuous bank for a road, especially this time of year when heavy runoff from the mountains flooded the banks. They were now only thirty miles from Montezuma Fort, but it looked like this could be the end of the trail for them.

Fortunately, there was a nice bench for camping, plenty of firewood, and no shortage of water, albeit muddy. On a low cliff overlooking the river, J. Smith and Wm. H. Hutchings left their names and the date "March 28, 1880."

If they could get to the top of Comb Ridge, then they might have a chance to complete the mission. The road crew went to work scraping, picking, and blasting yet another dugway through solid rock. After several days, a rough road was completed. Their teams of horses were exhausted, so as many as seven spans of horses were required to pull each heavy wagon up the slope. Some of the horses fell on their knees while the still erect ones were struggling against the grade. The men were forced to beat their jaded animals. Some of the horses had spasms. By the time all the wagons were on top, the trail was easily recognized by the dried blood and matted hair from the forelegs of the teams. One of

Figure 24. BUILDING A ROAD UP AND OVER COMB RIDGE AT SAN JUAN HILL WAS ONE OF THE MOST CHALLENGING PARTS OF THE ENTIRE JOURNEY.

Neilson's oxen keeled over dead in its yoke. And though a strong soul, whenever L. H. Redd Jr. recounted the story of San Juan Hill, he wept.

They struggled up San Juan Hill for the first three days of April. Near the top of the ridge, one of the pioneers carved "We Thank Thee Oh God," words from a popular Mormon hymn. The trail followed the ridge briefly, then drifted northeastward, where they encountered yet another steep-walled gulch—Butler Wash. They built another dugway, which they called the Jump, into and out of that canyon.

Figure 25. AERIAL VIEW OF COMB RIDGE AND THE SAN JUAN RIVER. THE BOTTOM ARROW POINTS AT WHERE THE WAGONS WENT UP SAN JUAN HILL. THE TOP ARROW IS AT THE ROAD CUT FOR HIGHWAY U.S. 163. BUTLER WASH IS THE LONG, SHADOWED GULCH COMING DOWN TO THE RIVER IN THE UPPER–RIGHT–HAND CORNER OF THE PHOTO.

Figure 26. "WE THANK THEE OH GOD" WAS INSCRIBED NEAR THE TOP OF SAN JUAN HILL.

They slowly rolled east, and by April 6, most of the outfits were camped on the flat river bottom next to Cottonwood Wash. Although Montezuma Fort was now less than twenty miles of easy travel away, they had lost their desire to go any farther. This would be their new home. At the suggestion of William Hutchings, it would be called Bluff City, though over time, the tiny settlement became known simply as Bluff.

✦ Following the Trail ✦

After reaching U.S. 163, it is possible to continue south down Comb Wash to San Juan Hill. In dry weather, the 4.3-mile track can be quite sandy, and in wet weather it is impossible to negotiate the flooded wash. USE CAUTION.

Another way to reach San Juan Hill is to take a San Juan River float trip. Besides seeing one of the most difficult sections of the wagon road, a trip down the San Juan River is renowned for its spectacular prehistoric rock art and dramatic geology, plus there are several fun rapids. The BLM's Monticello Field Office can provide a list of outfitters and the regulations regarding private river trips.

On the bench where the pioneers camped while building the road up San Juan Hill are signs of the prehistoric Anasazi, including some rock art, the depression of a great kiva, and, a short distance upstream, a well-preserved but extremely fragile cliff house. There are also ruins of the Hyde-Barton Trading Post and waterwheel. The trading post was built here to take advantage of north-south traffic crossing the river and east-west travelers on the Hole-in-the-Rock Trail. A prolonged argument with a couple of Navajo customers escalated to Amasa Barton being mortally wounded at his trading post in 1887.

Hike up San Juan Hill for a grand view and to see the pioneer inscription. To the northeast is private land, so return to the bench below.

By 1940, the old Indian trail up Navajo Hill and over Comb Ridge had been developed into a rough dirt road ascending in a series of tight, steep switchbacks. Highway 163 was further improved and finally paved through Comb Ridge in 1950.

Traveling on the modern road, it's easy to zoom across Butler Wash with hardly a glance. But for the pioneers' wagons, this relatively shallow canyon was yet another wearisome barrier. It is also the only geographic landmark along the trail named after a party member, John Butler from Panguitch. The pioneers' crossing was either about a third of a mile north of the modern highway or perhaps at some dugways about 3 miles north. Hobbs's inscription was located on May 14, 1960, but unfortunately it was destroyed when the contemporary highway was realigned.

Another 6 miles brings you to Bluff City.

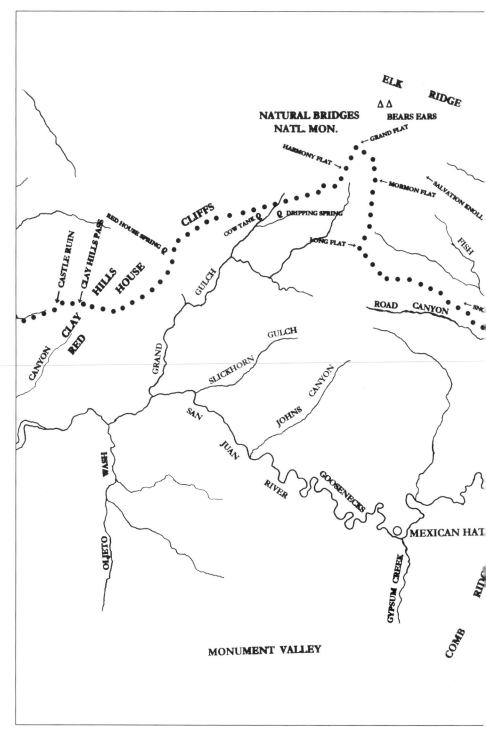

Map 5. Hole–in–the–Rock Trail, Grand Flat to Bluff.

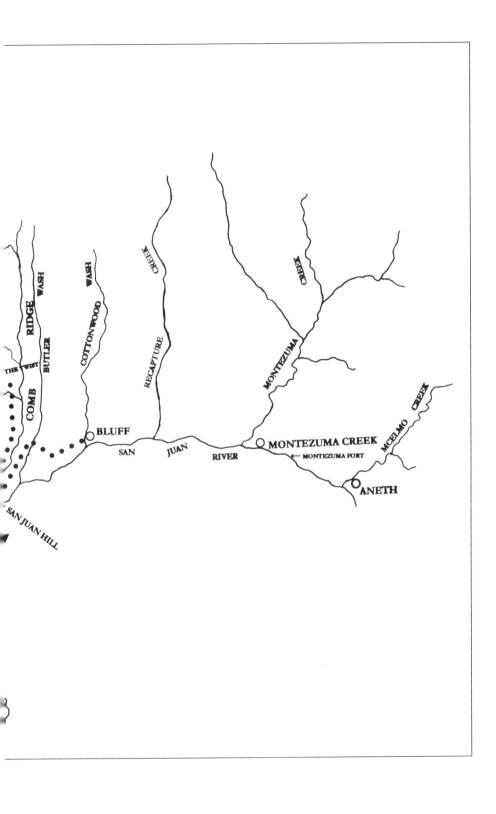

8

Bluff City
Since April 6, 1880, in Brief

*In making the 125 miles from Escalante the company had traveled 260
miles and had made 210 miles of new road through the most difficult
country wagons were ever taken through in all America.*

— Kumen Jones, a member of the San Juan Mission

No time was wasted laying off lots, building log cabins, and digging a
canal from the San Juan to irrigate fields. Because of limited suitable
land, a land lottery was held to determine who would stay in Bluff City
and who would move on to Montezuma Fort. About forty town lots
twelve rods square and forty field lots ranging from eight to twenty acres
were put in the lottery pot. Corn, sugarcane, wheat, oats, and barley
were planted, but floods made irrigation difficult.

Six days later, a son, Morris, was born to Emma and Nathaniel Alvin
Decker, the first birth in Bluff. About this time, President Silas S. Smith
returned from Salt Lake City. A few folks returned to Escalante to
retrieve livestock left there. That trip took only eight days!

On May 4 came the first death in Bluff. Roswell Stevens, one of the

Figure 27. Jens Nielson was appointed the first LDS bishop of Bluff City. Courtesy of the San Juan Historical Commission.

older members, died, apparently in part attributable to the rigors of the journey. He was buried in his wagon box due to lack of lumber.

On June 6, President Smith organized the Sunday school with James Decker as superintendent. Smith continued to preside over the San Juan Mission and as probate judge until being called two years later to move to the San Luis Valley of Colorado.

In late August, apostles Brigham Young Jr. and Erastus Snow visited and appointed Jens Nielson as bishop, with Lemuel H. Redd Jr. and Kumen Jones as his counselors.

But the colonists' troubles did not end. Beginning in December 1883, a series of snow and rainstorms pounded southeastern Utah. Heavy rains continued through spring 1884 when the runoff from the southern Rockies added to the San Juan's flow. The flood peaked on June 18. Houses in Bluff City were flooded and the irrigation system destroyed. All but one house at Montezuma Fort and most of the farmers' planted fields were washed away.

The residents of Bluff City asked to be released from their mission. Permission was granted, but those who would stay in Bluff City were told that they would be "doubly blessed of the Lord." Only a few families chose to leave.

When Francis Hammond became the San Juan Stake president in 1885, he urged a shift from farming, with its constant battle with the river, to ranching. This was an abandonment of Brigham Young's self-sufficiency economic philosophy of "home industry" in favor of an export economy dependent on national markets. But ranching rather than farming proved to be better suited for this area.

In sharp contrast to the floods of the 1880s, the 1890s proved to be a time of prolonged drought. Crops withered and cattle perished, but the people of Bluff City persisted. Many residents built large sandstone-block houses, an apparent commitment to the future.

A short-lived gold rush to San Juan River began during the winter of 1892–1893 and brought many prospectors through town, but few residents took part in it. A year later the boom had busted.

But life continued to be challenging in Bluff City. Eventually, most of the original families and their descendants moved away—many going north to start the farming and ranching communities of Verdure (1887), Monticello (1888), and Blanding (1905). By the 1920s, Bluff City was in further decline. The 1930 population was down to seventy. But after the uranium-prospecting boom and bust of the 1950s, new settlers began to discover the charms of Bluff City and southeastern Utah.

Today, Bluff is a quiet community of about three hundred souls. It has become an important tourist center for those wishing to "run the San Juan River," explore the numerous well-preserved archaeological sites, or visit the Navajo Nation, as well as a refuge for artists, writers, and retired scientists. Few are descended from those original emigrants, but, nonetheless, today's residents are fiercely proud of the pioneer heritage of this oasis in the desert.

Appendixes

In 1995, the Bluff City Historic District was entered into the *National Register of Historic Places.* An asterisk (*) denotes an original Bluff City settler.

STOP 1 ⊕ CEMETERY HILL AND THE BLUFF GREAT HOUSE. From the top of this bench, paved with ice-age river cobbles, one gets a nice overview of Bluff City and the surrounding countryside. Many of the original pioneers and their descendants are buried here. About halfway up the hill is the Bluff Great House, constructed between A.D. 900 and 1150 by the Anasazi and one of the northern-most Chacoan-style great houses. A prehistoric road and great kiva are associated with it. The adjacent kiosk explains more about this important archaeological site.

STOP 2 ⊕ JAMES DECKER HOUSE (1898).* James and Anna Marie Decker and their eleven children lived here. Their daughter Lena Deseret was born at Fiftymile Camp, January 3, 1880. Tragically, James and four of the children died from diphtheria during the winter of 1900-1901.

STOP 3 ⊕ LEMUEL REDD JR. HOUSE (LATE 1890s).* Redd was San Juan County's first tax assessor.

STOP 4 ⊕ HYRUM PERKINS HOUSE (1890s).* Hyrum Perkins and his brother Benjamin were miners from Wales and supervised the drilling and blasting to build the Hole-in-the-Rock Road.

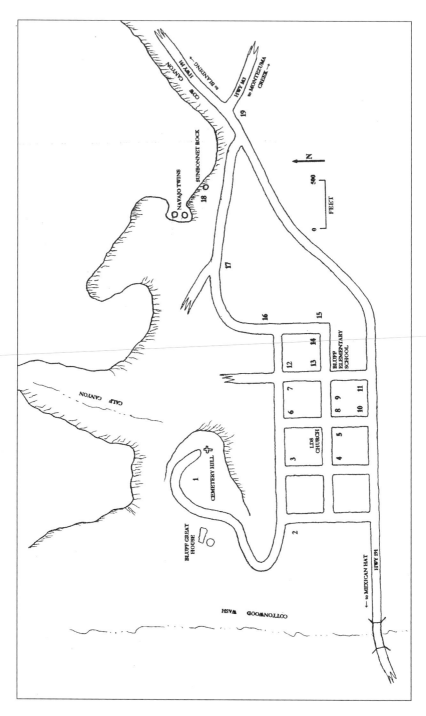

Map 6. Bluff City walking tour.

STOP 5 ✟ BLUFF SCHOOL AND JAIL (1896). Once an imposing two-story structure, the old school has seen many different uses through time. Only a corner of the original building exists today, but original window arches can still be seen even though the windows have been bricked in.

STOP 6 ✟ PLATTE LYMAN HOUSE (1890s).* Not one who was keen on rough pioneer life, Lyman must have enjoyed this elegant house. He served as county prosecuting attorney, as stake president, and later as president over the European Mission.

STOP 7 ✟ WILLARD BUTT HOUSE (CA. 1897).* Note that this pioneer house is constructed of lumber, not sandstone blocks. Butt opened a sawmill near Verdure in 1881 and operated the first steam-powered sawmill in the county ten years later. One exterior wall contains part of his wagon.

STOP 8 ✟ KUMEN JONES HOUSE RUINS (1880s OR '90s).* This house had some of most elegant stonework in Bluff City.

STOP 9 ✟ MEETINGHOUSE REPLICA. This type of log building was used as a school, church, dance hall, and gathering place until 1894. Next door is the future site of a replica of the original Co-op Store, which will house a Hole-in-the-Rock museum. The Co-op Store, built in 1882, was the first store in Bluff City.

STOP 10 ✟ JOSEPH BARTON CABIN (1880–1897).* This is the oldest pioneer building still standing. Joined cabins were part of a fort built in 1880, with a well inside to provide community water.

STOP 11 ✟ JANE AND JOHN ALLAN HOUSE (CA. 1885). The remaining stone section is only a third of the original house. The Allans moved to Bluff City after losing their home in Montezuma Fort during the 1884 floods.

Figure 28. THE BLUFF CITY MEETINGHOUSE WAS COMPLETED IN THE FALL OF 1880 AND SERVED FOR FOURTEEN YEARS AS A CHURCH, SCHOOL, DANCE HALL, AND PUBLIC MEETING PLACE. BLUFF SETTLERS ARE PICTURED (LEFT TO RIGHT): PLATTE D. LYMAN, KUMEN JONES, JENS NIELSON, JAMES B. DECKER, AND FRANCIS HAMMOND. COURTESY OF THE SAN JUAN HISTORICAL COMMISSION.

Figure 29. THE JENS NIELSON FOUR GABLES HOUSE IN BLUFF BEING LOVINGLY RESTORED.

STOP 12 ✦ Jens Nielson Four Gables House and Mill (early 1890s).* This brick house was where Jens Nielson's first wife, Elsie Rasmussen Nielson, lived. She is credited with planting the first mulberry trees in Bluff City.

STOP 13 ✦ Jens Nielson House (1880s).* Jens Nielson was the first LDS bishop of Bluff City. His second wife, Kristin Jensen Nielson, lived in this house next door to his other wife.

STOP 14 ✦ Calf Canyon Bed and Breakfast (1997). Although the B&B is relatively new, the house was designed to look similar to the historic houses. The northeast corner of the house incorporates a masonry remnant of the old Twin Rocks Market.

STOP 15 ✦ Frederick Joseph Adams House (1890s). Adams arrived in Bluff City as a child with his parents in 1882.

STOP 16 ✦ John Albert Scorup House (1904). Scorup built this house when a number of Bluff City residents were moving north to Blanding or Monticello. He was a partner in the Scorup-Summerville Cattle Company, which grazed cattle on a two million-acre range that extended from the confluence of the Colorado and San Juan northeast to the Blue Mountains. While he lived half the year out on the range, his wife and six daughters enjoyed the comforts of town life.

STOP 17 ✦ Nick Lovace House (mid-1890s). Lovace was the stonemason who built many of the stone houses in Bluff City and Blanding. His house may have originally resembled the Jens Nielson House, but was rebuilt after a fire destroyed the second story.

STOP 18 ✦ Navajo Twins and Sunbonnet Rock. Twin sandstone pillars tower over the Twin Rocks Trading Post and Restaurant. Between the buildings on the fanciful, balanced Sunbonnet Rock, the Sons of Utah Pioneers have mounted a commemorative plaque to the San Juan Mission.

Figure 30. THE NAVAJO TWINS AND SUNBONNET ROCK IN BLUFF. THERE IS A PLAQUE COMMEMORATING THE SAN JUAN MISSION JUST UNDER THE CAPSTONE OF SUNBONNET ROCK.

STOP 19 ✦ COW CANYON TRADING POST AND RESTAURANT (POST-WORLD WAR II). An eclectic place constructed by Rusty Musselman, one-time sheriff of the county who said he didn't design an old building, he just used old things that he found. In 1970 when the Utah State Board of Education decided to produce a film about the San Juan Mission, Musselman furnished props. Many of the actors were descendants of the Hole-in-the-Rock pioneers.

~ For More Information ~

Anasazi Indian State Park
P.O. Box 1429
Boulder, UT 84716–1429
435.335.7308

Bluff City Historic Preservation
  Association
P.O. Box 76
Bluff City, UT 84512

Bryce Canyon National Park
Bryce Canyon, UT 84717
435.834.5322

Bureau of Land Management
Escalante Field Office
755 West Main
P.O. Box 225
Escalante, UT 84726
435.826.5600

Bureau of Land Management
Monticello Field Office
P.O. Box 7
Monticello, UT 84535
435.587.1532
http://www.ut.blm.gov/monticello

Bureau of Land Management
Price Field Office
125 South 600 West
Price, UT 84501
435.636.3600
http://www.ut.blm.gov/price

Capitol Reef National Park
HC-70, Box 15
Torrey, UT 84775–9602
435.425.3791

Dixie National Forest
Forest Supervisor's Office
82 North 100 East
P.O. Box 0627
Cedar City, UT 84721–0627
435.865.3200

Dixie National Forest
Escalante Ranger District
755 West Main
P.O. Box 246
Escalante, UT 84726
435.826.5400

Dixie National Forest
Powell Ranger District
225 East Center
P.O. Box 80
Panguitch, UT 84759
435.676.8815

Escalante Petrified Forest
  State Park
P.O. Box 350
Escalante, UT 84726–0350
435.826.4466

Glen Canyon National
    Recreation Area
Escalante Ranger Station
P.O. Box 511
Escalante, UT 84726
435.826.5651
http://www.nps.gov/glca/hitr.htm

Grand Staircase-Escalante
    National Monument
Escalante Interagency Visitor and
Recreation Information Center
P.O. Box 225
755 West Main
Escalante, UT 84726
435.826.5499
escalant@ut.blm.gov
http://www.ut.blm.gov/monument

Hole-in-the-Rock Foundation
P.O. Box 1053
Monticello, UT 84535
435.587.2484

Natural Bridges National
    Monument
HC-60, Box 1
Lake Powell, UT 84533-0101
435.692.1234

San Juan Historical Commission
24 South 300 West
Blanding, UT 84511

Maps

Besides the excellent USGS 7.5-minute topographic quads, the *Indian Country Guide Map* published by the Automobile Club of Southern California is very useful and available at many shops and visitor centers in the area. The BLM's *Arizona Strip District Visitor Map 1993* is helpful for following the exploratory party's route across Buckskin Mountain (the Honeymoon Trail) in Arizona. And the Dixie National Forest maps are handy, too.

Bibliography

Aton, James M., and Robert S. McPherson. *River Flowing from the Sunrise: An Environmental History of the Lower San Juan.* Logan: Utah State University Press, 2000.

Bagley, Will. *Blood of the Prophets: Brigham Young and the Massacre at Mountain Meadows.* Norman: University of Oklahoma Press, 2002.

Brooks, Juanita. *The Mountain Meadows Massacre.* Norman: University of Oklahoma Press, 1962.

Chesher, Greer K. *Heart of the Desert Wild: Grand Staircase-Escalante National Monument.* Bryce Canyon, Utah: Bryce Canyon Natural History Association, 2000.

Crabtree, Lamont. *The Incredible Mission.* N.p., 1980.

———. *Journey of the San Juan Colonizers: Hole-in-the-Rock Expedition Multi-Image Documentary.* Produced by Lamont Crabtree. 1995. Videocassette.

Crampton, C. Gregory. *Ghosts of Glen Canyon: History beneath Lake Powell.* St. George, Utah: Publishers Place, 1986.

Crampton, C. Gregory, and Steven K. Madsen. *In Search of the Spanish Trail.* Salt Lake City: Gibbs Smith Publisher, 1994.

Crampton, C. Gregory, and Dwight L. Smith, eds. *The Hoskininni Papers: Mining in Glen Canyon, 1897-1902,* by Robert B. Stanton. University of Utah Anthropological Papers no. 54, Glen Canyon Series 15 (November). Salt Lake City: University of Utah Press, 1961.

Elkins, Richard Ira. *The Honeymoon Trail: A Pioneer Story for Young People.* Salt Lake City: Specialty Press, 1987.

Fleischner, Thomas Lowe. *Singing Stone: A Natural History of the Escalante Canyons.* Salt Lake City: University of Utah Press, 1999.

Hill, Linda M., ed. *Learning from the Land: Grand Staircase-Escalante National Monument Science Symposium Proceedings.* Copies available from Bureau of Land Management, Utah State Office, Salt Lake City. Washington, D.C.: U.S. Government Printing Office, 1999.

Hurst, Winston, Owen Severance, and Dale Davidson. "Uncle Albert's Ancient Roads." *Blue Mountain Shadows* 12 (summer 1993): 2-9.

Jones, Raymond Smith. "Last Wagon through the Hole-in-the-Rock." *Desert Magazine* (June 1954): 22-25.

Kelsey, Michael R. *Boater's Guide to Lake Powell.* Provo: Kelsey Publishing, 1989.

Knipmeyer, James H. *Butch Cassidy Was Here: Historic Inscriptions of the Colorado Plateau.* Salt Lake City: University of Utah Press, 2002.

Kosik, Fran. *Native Roads: The Complete Motoring Guide to the Navajo and Hopi Nations.* Flagstaff: Creative Solutions Publishing, 1996.

McDonald, Ron. "Fort Montezuma." *Blue Mountain Shadows* 30 (summer 2004): 10–56.

McPherson, Robert S. *A History of San Juan County: In the Palm of Time.* Salt Lake City: Utah State Historical Society, 1995.

Miller, David E. *Hole-in-the-Rock: An Epic in the Colonization of the Great American West.* Salt Lake City: University of Utah Press, 1966.

Netoff, Dennis I., Brian J. Cooper, and Ralph R. Shroba. "Giant Sandstone Weathering Pits near Cookie Jar Butte, Southeastern Utah." *Proceedings of the Second Biennial Conference on Research in Colorado Plateau National Parks* (1995): 25–53.

Perkins, Cornelia Adams, Marian Gardner Nielson, and Lenora Butt Jones. *Saga of San Juan.* Salt Lake City: Mercury Publishing, 1968.

Powell, Allan Kent. *San Juan County: People, Resources, and History.* Salt Lake City: Utah State Historical Society, 1983.

Reay, Lee. *Incredible Passage through the Hole-in-the-Rock.* Provo: Meadow Lane Publications, 1980.

Rusho, W. L. *Everett Ruess: A Vagabond for Beauty.* Salt Lake City: Peregrine Smith, 1983.

Rusho, W. L., and C. Gregory Crampton. *Desert River Crossing: Historic Lee's Ferry on the Colorado River.* Salt Lake City: Peregrine Smith, 1981.

Sanchez, Joseph P. *Explorers, Traders, and Slavers: Forging the Old Spanish Trail, 1678–1850.* Salt Lake City: University of Utah Press, 1997.

Topping, Gary. *Glen Canyon and the San Juan Country.* Moscow: University of Idaho Press, 1997.

Warner, Ted J., ed. *The Domínguez-Escalante Journal: Their Expedition through Colorado, Utah, Arizona, and New Mexico in 1776.* Salt Lake City: University of Utah Press, 1995.

Young, Norma Perkins. *Anchored Lariats on the San Juan Frontier.* Provo: Community Press, 1985.